Dearest Jean,
  I was in
the Charity Shop yesterday
and spotted this book
on Well Dressing.
Hope you enjoy.
  Love Ina

WELL DRESSING

Peter Naylor & Lindsey Porter

Buxton Well Dressing, 1863

Above: Awaiting the clay, Hall Well, Tissington, 1997

Opposite page: Youlgreave, 1997

WELL
DRESSING

Peter Naylor & Lindsey Porter

Landmark Publishing Ltd

═══ Published by ═══

Ashbourne Hall, Cokayne Ave,
Ashbourne, Derbyshire, DE6 1EJ, England
Tel: (01335) 347349 Fax: (01335) 347303
e-mail: landmark@clara.net
web site: www.landmarkpublishing.co.uk

1st edition

ISBN 1 84306 023 X

© **Peter Naylor & Lindsey Porter 2002**

British Library Cataloguing in Publication Data: a catalogue
record for this book is available from the British Library.

Printed by CPI, Bookcraft, Midsomer Norton, Somerset

Design & reproduction by James Allsopp

Cover captions:

Front cover; Bakewell, Bath Gardens, 2000; *Insert:* Tideswell, 2000

Back cover; *Left top:* Petalling, Tissington: *Middle:* Treading clay, Tissington, both 1997;
Top right: Youlgreave, 2000. *Main Photograph:* Hand's Well, Tissington, 1998

The publishers wish to acknowledge the assistance of:
Jane Allen; Bridget Ardley; Barbara, Edward & Margaret Carr; Dorothy Crookes; Jennie Dullage; P Finch; Bryan
Harris; Hartington Primary School; John Howard; Don Hughes; Christine Jones; Lichfield Heritage Centre and
Laura; Charlotte Linsell; Eileen MacAskill; Sara Maslauskas; Michael Miller; Caroline Parsons; Mr V B Peirson; Anne
Slater; Mike Smith; Carole Unwin; Christine Wheeldon; Derek Wigley

CONTENTS

When I inherited the Tissington Estate from my late uncle in 1989 little did I realise what a large part Well-Dressings would play in the rest of my life! Now, each year, I am involved from the start in preparations for our annual event which takes place in the week following Ascension Day. I find myself caught up in such diverse jobs as the production of the guide leaflet, the hiring of the mobile loos for the week, the digging and puddling of the clay, the intricate pricking out of the pictures and the dressings of the actual wells themselves! The six wells dressed in Tissington every year are the culmination of a huge amount of planning, preparation and hard work by the friends and inhabitants of the village. Often people make a pilgrimage to Tissington every year solely to assist, in whatever way, in the creation of the Well-Dressings – and it is estimated that each well takes 200 work hours to complete. There is huge satisfaction in our small village on the Wednesday evening when, once again, we have completed this enormous task and all the wells are erected. The knowledge, too, that the wells will be visited by around 50,000 people in the ensuing seven days, gives great pleasure to us all.

Peter Naylor and Lindsey Porter's beautifully photographed record explains the full process of the dressing of the wells from the first tractor load of clay to the completed floral collage. Since my involvement, I have received enquiries from all over the world; from Canada to Australia, from Wales to Germany, about our celebration and how and why we create these wonderful tributes in flowers. The sense of community and camaraderie that the whole process evokes is of such special importance to a village like ours, that I trust Well-Dressings will continue for as long as wells flow freely. Not only is the event about the life-giving water, it is also about a life-enhancing spirit of community. I trust that you will enjoy reading it and that it will encourage you to visit a Well Dressing in person – I can assure you that it will inspire you.

Sir Richard FitzHerbert Bt
Tissington Hall
March 2002

Hand's Well, Tissington, 1998

Tideswell, 2000; detail of the centre panel showing Wells Cathedral from the Bishop's Palace Moat. It was designed by Paul Fletcher

As far as the authors are aware, this is the first book to address the history of well dressing. There are and have been many colour booklets and leaflets which satisfy the curiosity of visitors but nothing to help the serious student of the subject and the more enquiring visitor.

By visitors we mean those who visit the well dressings every year to enjoy their beauty and to take part in the local events which usually attend the dressing festivals. In so saying, one automatically assumes that we are talking of Derbyshire in general and the Peak District of Derbyshire in particular. Indeed, most leaflets which are published each year for the benefit of the visitor refer to well dressing as being unique to this county. This is not true. Well dressing is practised throughout the kingdom and beyond, but admittedly, it has achieved its greatest popularity in Derbyshire mostly because the tradition is especially strong here and the heights of this decorative art have reached their apogee here also.

This book will examine the origins of the tradition and look at the various places where well dressing is still practised. One problem facing the authors was the tracking of the history of each well dressing, for records were not always kept for the majority of the wells and only a few wells are very well recorded, for example those at Tissington.

We would also like to clear up the confusion suffered by many a visitor who is puzzled by what is meant by a well. The terms well and spring are synonymous and re-used throughout the history of the British Isles to mean the same thing, witness the Domesday Survey. There are numerous place names which in-corporate the word well but not the word spring. To name but a few; Blackwell (dark water), Whitwell (white water), Etwall (Etta's well).

This book also includes what we would like to think is the first definitive list of known wells which are dressed. In so doing we have been mindful that certain of these are sporadic and others now defunct. These have been included for historical accuracy and in the hope that they may be dressed more regularly and might be revived.

"Special" years attract a revival of well dressing such as has happened in the following recent years:

1951 Festival of Britain
1953 Coronation of Queen Elizabeth II
1977 Queen Elizabeth II Silver Jubilee
2000 The Millennium

The other aspect of well dressing which puzzles the visitor is the lack of a well or spring. Due to the increase in the number of dressings over the last ten years, people have taken to siting a dressing at places other than wells. One must appreciate their

St Ann's Well, Buxton, c. 1920

enthusiasm in this although it does cause some criticism from the long established dressers who would not dream of building such a monument other than near to water. This distinction has been made in the itinerary in this book. Many of the dressings date from the time of Queen Victoria when piped supplies were laid into villages for which benefaction the inhabitants dressed the taps rather than the wells. Well dressing is therefore often referred to as tap dressing. Some of these were gifted by the Lord of the Manor (Pilsley), some were supplied by a village committee or company (Youlgreave).

This lack of information about certain wells has created problems in the writing of this book. Therefore, the authors have chosen to deal with the well documented dressings in some detail and for those poorly recorded we have addressed in geographical areas.

We are also aware that there will be dressings not included in this book, due to the possibility of new ones being undertaken as we publish. For this please accept our apologies and in such cases we ask that you advise the publisher to allow the details to be included in a future edition if the demand warrants it.

The reader is encouraged to visit some of these dressings to enjoy the skill and artistry shown by the various tableaux. The reader is also encouraged to call in at the dressing stage to see how it is done and some dressers encourage newcomers to have a try for themselves. This way a greater appreciation of the dressings is enjoyed, for it is a painstaking and time-consuming process. One can therefore appreciate the anger suffered by the dressers when their work is vandalized, as sometimes happens.

Finally, the vexed question which is often raised: "*Which are the best wells to visit*". The authors apologize for not answering this, for it would be unreasonable to take sides in this. Indeed, even the authors cannot agree as to which are the best dressings because we have both been involved for some years (Peter Naylor: a dresser and Lindsey Porter: photographer) and naturally we are partisan in the matter. We would both agree though, that a visit to the Tissington dressings would be worthwhile! Some dressings are certainly below par but these may be newcomers to the art and in a few years will probably rank equal with the best. And of course allowances must be made for the efforts of the children, these will be the dressers of the future and are to be applauded for continuing the tradition long after we have all gone.

Porter and Naylor, 2002

Warmbrook Well, Wirksworth 1955

The Mirror

OF

LITERATURE, AMUSEMENT, AND INSTRUCTION.

834.]   SATURDAY, MAY 20, 1837.   [PR

WELL-FLOWERING IN DERBYSHIRE.

LET THE
FOUNTAINS
BE DISPERSED
ABROAD
AND RIVERS OF
WATERS IN THE
STREETS

WELL AT TISSINGTON.

Why water rather than any other natural phenomena?

This must surely be due to the essential part water plays in our everyday lives and its importance to the continuation of life. Our earliest ancestors always chose a location for their settlements near to water. Our bodies are constituted of 90% water. Over half of the surface of the world is covered with water. It is essential to our wellbeing and has been ritualized by religions the world over, for example baptism in the Christian tradition.

Some argue that offering votive gifts to springs came with the Romans. This is unlikely as one would expect the tradition to live on over what was the Roman Empire, particularly in Italy. We could only find one similar activity south of Rome at Genzano where a huge pattern of flowers is laid on the road through the village. Dr Laura Oliveti reports "not on a board as in Derbyshire." (1) The Romans did not occupy either the Highlands of Scotland or Ireland but wells are still dressed here in their original form.

It was, however, common with the Romans and Greeks, the former had the Goddess Fontanalia in honour of the Nymphs of the wells and streams. (2)

The "original form" is when the wells were decorated, if that is the word, by tying pieces of rag to the boughs of trees which overhang or are close to the water. This is personified by the "Cloutie" wells of Scotland, a cloutie being a piece of rag as in "clout rags" and similar wells in Ireland.

It is known that the Celts (late Iron Age) in Britain venerated certain trees, rocks and water. They had sprites associated with the wells, two of the most famous in Britain being Sulis and Artemis, both of which were adopted by the Romans when naming Bath in Somerset and Buxton in Derbyshire,

Above; Left: Hall Well, Tissington, 1863 (from The Book of Days, 1864); Right: Hall Well in Edwardian times

Opposite page: The oldest known illustration of a dressed well, 1837

Hand's Well, Tissington, early 20th Century

Aqua Sulis and Aqua Arnemetia. Later Sulis was linked with a Roman god to make Sulis Minerva. Arnemetia's name comes from are(e) meaning "in front of" and nemeton for "a grove (of trees)", a strong Celtic place.(3) The Romans built a temple on the site along with a bath house, the latter being the famous bath still in existence. Significantly these are the only two springs in the country that have thermal water by definition – the temperature of the water must be higher than the average annual air temperature surrounding the spring. With global warming, these claims are under threat long term. (4)

The attribution of St Anne to the Buxton springs echoes the water sprite Santan. There are numerous such springs along with those named St Helen after the sprite Elen. (5) It is noted that these sprites along with many others were always female, a tradition with other cultures also. This is probably why today we frequently have a well queen. The reasons the Romans originally left the Celts alone to get on with their druidically based religion was acceptable as it kept the "natives" happy as it were. However, Paulinus in 61 AD destroyed the cult of the Druids completely.

When the Christianisation of Britain was started, this cult also went along with the more harmless traditions amongst the Celts, and as part of making this new religion acceptable, they built their early churches, especially the Saxon ones on existing holy sites which were often springs or with springs close by.

Following the joining of the Celtic Church with the Roman Church, a different view was taken of these practices. A Canon by the Second Council of Arles, 1425 declared, "If in the territory of a Bishop, infidels light torches or venerate trees, fountains or stones, and he neglects to abolish this usage, he must know that he is guilty of sacrilege". A Draconian stance to take, which suggests that these customs were still rife and continued to be so for, in the 7th century, Pope Gregory instructed St Augustine to adapt sacred sites for the use of the church. However this seemed not to have solved the perceived problem for over the next few centuries, several edicts were issued to denounce the practices of the worship of "the sun or the moon, fire or flood, wells or stones, or any kind of forest tree". Do we not still revere these things, if only sub-consciously?

Even as recent as the time of Henry VIII, his Lord Chancellor, Thomas Cromwell was instructing the destruction of the paraphernalia of well worship. At Buxton, Sir William Bassett destroyed a statue of St Anne along with all discarded crutches and sticks. This was short lived as Mary Queen of Scots, whilst captive in Derbyshire, enjoyed visiting Buxton to take the waters to ease her rheumatism. On her visits she would have noticed the accumulation of votive offerings left by pilgrims usually in the form of effigies of the diseased part of the body. At times of the great pestilence, the Bubonic Plague, such visits could do no harm when compared with the ever present threat of death by the hideous Black Death which it is reckoned took the lives of about half of the total population of Europe including Britain.

If the practice of well dressing had supposedly been destroyed by various agencies, well worship seems to have lived on. Our earliest reference of dressing wells in modern times is 1348/9 at Tissington, Derbyshire. A reference to a sum of money being paid for dressing a well at Repton in 1666 is probably an instruction to tidy the stone enclosure. (6)

References:

1) *The History and Topography of Ashbourne and the Valley of the Dove*, Anon, 1839

2) *Shenley Court School and Sixth Form Centre. 24.12.01*
   Newton S, Boyd M, Palmer M.

3) *Some notes on St Anne's Well at Buxton,* Morrell R.W., Mercian Mysteries, No 18, February 1994

4) *Ancient Wells and Springs of Derbyshire,* Naylor P J., Cromford, 1983

5) *ibid*

6) This reference is unconfirmed, but is believed to come from a reference in *History and Topographical Description of Repton,* 1854, referring to the Constable's account for the Restoration.

Two early 20th Century views of Tissington wells:
Yew Tree Well (left), Coffin Well (below)

Tissington seems to have always adopted a
religious theme in the dressing of its wells

It seems provocative to name certain dressings as being better than the others and this interpretation should not be applied the those represented in this chapter. The four dressings addressed here have a long tradition compared to those which have lapsed or are recent starters. They are undeniably excellent, much visited but most importantly, they are better documented than most.

They also boast more than one well dressed at any one time, indeed Wirksworth have had up to fourteen on show in the 1990s. The fame of the Tissington dressings is widespread and with good reason are they chosen as the definitive expression of this art.

Tissington, Hand's Well, 1975

Wirksworth, Well by St Mary's Gate, 2000

Youlgreave, 2000

Tideswell, 2000

Tissington

Ascension Day

Tissington is a charming estate village, the Hall being the home for centuries of the FitzHerberts, who are the Lords of the Manor.

Here they dress genuine springs, which still issue water, which is used by the villagers should the piped supply fail. To add to the attraction most of the springs are set off by masonry surrounds and features.

It has often been said that all Derbyshire dressings commenced here in 1348-9 as a thank you after the village escaped the dreadful infestation known as the Black Death (Bubonic Plague or the Pestilence). This had reached its zenith in these years, having ravaged the local villages but left Tissington unharmed, except possibly one person who might have succumbed. The villagers believed that the purity of the water was the reason. They were indeed fortunate to evade the disease, which medically would not have been because of the water, but more likely due to their comparative isolation. The Black Death respected nobody as the story of Eyam's sacrifice will testify. A second claim for the origin of well dressing in this village dates from the year 1615, when a severe drought was experienced. At Youlgreave the parish register records that between the 25th March 1615 and August, 1615 only three showers of rain fell. When the surrounding villages were rendered waterless, Tissington alone enjoyed a plentiful supply of water. This, if true, may have been a revival of the custom. One should remember the dependence in those days on natural water supplies.

The antiquity of the well dressing here owes much to the FitzHerbert family, who still show considerable interest in the custom; the current incumbent, Sir Richard FitzHerbert helps with the puddling of the clay amongst other activities.

In 1748, Nicholas Hardinge, the Clerk of the House of Commons recorded that:
"At Tissington, FitzHerbert's village, we saw springs adorned with garlands; in one of these was a tablet inscribed with rhymes, composed by the schoolmaster in honour of the fountains, which, as FitzHerbert informs me are annually commemorated upon Holy Thursday, the minister with his parishioners praying and singing over them." (6)

The earliest known written evidence refers to the wells nearest to the church being dressed in 1758. A description of 1817 makes it clear that the wells were dressed according to a design, unusually the boards being made each year rather than reusing them every year as is the custom today. This might suggest that the formalised method now used was already in use, and if this is the case, this is also the oldest mention of the custom in its present form on record. Therefore, Tissington may well be the oldest dressings in the county. The Hall Well was not included at this time due to the difficulty in dressing a well having an arched alcove.

It is apparent that these dressings were popular with Ashbourne folk: "who were keen to get a lift on a horse, or anything that pulled, in order to get there with the least inconvenience." (4) The social aspect of the festivity appears to have been high in their minds also. The Reverend Ward wrote in 1827, that after the blessing of the wells:
"The people then disperse to their respective dwellings, which, as there is but one small public house in the village, are freely open to all, and the day is concluded with the utmost hospitality and festivity."

This was confirmed in 1839, when it was stated in a local paper that the design was in the form of a picture, specifically stating that:
"The stems and flowers are closely inserted, and a brilliant mosaic is thus prepared, forming as it were, a ground work for various ornamented designs, as crowns and stars, and appropriate mottoes, chiefly from scripture, which are most imperiously introduced."

This also tells us that quotations from the Bible were being used for a theme and petalling may be in use. He also reported that the dressings comprised the fixing in of flowers in soft clay spread on boards. After the church service there was a procession to all five wells where there was a reading of an epistle or psalm and a hymn sung to the sound of musical instruments, possibly the church band.

William Adam commented that even Sir Henry FitzHerbert: "Very literally throws open his old Hall to all comers upon such occasions". Surprisingly this gratuitous hospitality was maintained through virtually the whole of the nineteenth century. As late as 1880, it was reported that "Open house was kept by everyone according to their means and all comers are received with welcome." Whilst similar hospitality was evident at Tideswell, Wirksworth, Bakewell and elsewhere, it was reported that "in no place is it so heartily carried out as at Tissington." (5)

Sixty years later an article in The Mirror newspaper added that the remainder of the day was spent in rural sports and holiday pastimes, whatever these were! The same paper described the dressings of 1836 and included the first known illustration of a well dressing. It also included a description made in 1817 originally from Brayley's Graphic and Historical Illustrations, which tells us, "The well that pleased me most, was one that stood in a retired garden, it had an arbour formed from trees with wreaths of laburnum, and the common blue hare-bells thrown over, at the top was a figure of Pity, (holding a medallion of the King), bending to Hygeia, with her accustomed offerings of fox gloves. The drapery of the figures defied all description, the colours were so well chosen. On the right hand of Pity was a globe most exquisitely designed: upon one part you might see the word "England" on the left a ship with all her sails hoisted: on the figure were the crown and the words, "God save the King", in sweet-briar leaves upon a ground of lilacs. For many weeks before Holy Thursday (which this year happened on May 4), the inhabitants are busily gathering moss, flowers, etc and arranging the framework for their forthcoming festival. Indeed, throughout the year they are thinking of new designs and arrangements, concerning which the most profound secrecy is observed among the half-dozen or more determined to dress their own appropriate well. That it is a work of time and reflection is apparent, when we come to consider the antiquity of the custom, the many previous patterns and the wish to procure new and striking designs, as floral holiday attracts immense numbers to the otherwise quiet village on the day in question, and is looked forward to with anxiety by all Derbyshire folks; as it is one of the old customs of England that, unlike others, seems to strengthen rather than decline by age – a circumstance highly creditable to the taste of people, and gratifying to every lover of pastoral beauty, which in this instance shines forth superior to any other country custom, the Maypole itself excluded." This sentiment could equally apply today.

His engraving represents one of these wells, sketched on the festival of 12 May 1836, by a young friend:

"Who visited the floral fete, and who was, like myself, enthusiastic on the subject, but, notwithstanding his anticipations of the scene, he confessed that 'it exceeded in beauty anything that can be said in praise of it.' A circumstance that seldom happens in our matter-of-fact times, when simple elegancies of life are driven out of sight by fashionable and affected imitation of nature on the one hand and the gloomy mammon of trade on the other.

The beauty of the well represented by the engraving, (which is the first that has ever been in print), cannot be fully appreciated by a mere glance, unless the reader is made fully aware of the labour bestowed upon it, which is more than any casual observer would give credit for. The whole front of the building, pillars, brick-work, inscriptions, those parts left white in the cut, or those tinted, were all formed of flowers, and stood about eight feet in height, by five feet in breadth. It was the design of a female, and occupied her more than a week, although assisted by five other persons, some working by night as others did by day. The inscriptions in this instance seemed to me to be particularly well chosen; the bountiful supply indicated by the poetical description was, in phrase, extremely pleasing, while the extract from the Proverbs in the centre, in its profuse benevolence could only be fully appreciated by combining it, in idea, with a parching eastern clime, in allusion to which it was spoken.

If the reader would again look at the Cut, and follow me in Description, I think as accurate an idea of the original may be had, as it is in this instance practicable to obtain. The upper triangle portion, represented as white, was formed of buttercups and cowslips, bordered with moss, and the wreath of laurel leaves. The inscription immediately under it ('In every form, etc') was formed of holly-berries, on a ground of blue harebells. The pillars at the sides had alternate square patches of blue, red and yellow flowers from top to bottom; while the arched front was made to represent

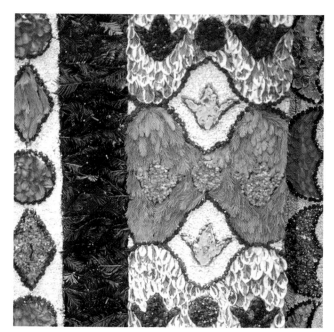

Above left: Town Well, 1975; Above right: A close-up of the petaller's art at Tissington, 1998; Right: Detail of Yew Tree Well (see opposite also)

brick-work, being a solid mass of red daisies. With the white lines marking the courses of the layers, formed from wood emery (anemone). The inscription within the recess had a white ground of daisies, the letters were formed of the blue-bell petals, the vases, blue, red and yellow, of different flowers, were on a ground of bright, green moss. In front of the posts and chains, also covered the moss; and the low wall bounding the whole was formed also of flowers, disposed in the same manner as the imitation brick-work above. This enclosed plants and flowers; and the small central bush was so arranged over the well that the water was conveyed through small pipes that passed down each pendulous branch, and a unique fountain was the result seeming to spout forth from the leaves of the living tree. The sides of the building, (if I may so term it), were supported by bunches of holly and laburnum, and thus was completed the picturesque design."

By the end of the nineteenth century, well dressing seems to have taken a knock. In 1891, it was recorded that "the spiritual character and quaint simplicity of well dressings is maintained only at Tissington. Well dressings elsewhere in Derbyshire have degenerated." (7)

The date of this dressing can cause problems. In conversation with a dresser, one learns that "If Ascsention day is early and the weather has been bad we really suffer". Suitable materials, especially flowers, can be in short supply. (8)

The dressings here therefore, are at least 6-700 years old and as far as one can ascertain were interrupted only for the two World Wars of the 20th Century and in 2001 due to the outbreak of Foot and Mouth Disease.

The wells (springs) are:

Town Well

This is located at the eastern end of the village on the road to Bradbourne "splash" – a well known local ford. Whilst the other wells are ornamental, this one is purely practical having a squat square shape with a pent roof. (9)

Coffin Well

Originally Frith's Well, named after a tenant farmer whose farm was close to the well. (1). It comprises a large stone cistern located in a garden behind a gate by the post office. The cistern is shaped like a giant's coffin, hence its name.

Yew Tree Well

Originally Goodwin's Well, also named after a tenant farmer whose farm was close to the well. This stands at the side of the main road at the western edge gate to the village with a horseshoe shaped structure of local stone.

Hand's Well

This is in the form of an oval basin at the head of the village under a cottage wall. Named after the Hand's family of Overfields Farm, the cottage behind the well.

Hall Well

Originally known as St Helen's Well, this being ascribed to Lord St Helens, brother of the first baronet of Tissington, Sir William FitzHerbert. Alternatively it could have been named after St Helen as are so many springs in the British Isles. St Helen, the mother of Alexander the Great, is associated with water. She was canonised after finding the true cross in a rock cistern. Elen or Elan was also a Celtic water sprite and is honoured under the guise of St Helen.

This well was also known as the Cup and Saucer Well for a period. (2) It faces Tissington Hall and is an imposing structure having an overhanging arch with three basins over which the water flows from one side to the other before it collects in a small rivulet which channels the water to the village pond.(9)

1) Derby Advertiser 09.05.1947
2) Baddeley M J
3) *Ashbourne and the Valley of the Dove*, Anon, 1839
4) Derbyshire Courier 1829
5) Ditto 1880
6) *Old English Customs* p49
7) *Pictures of the Peak*, Bradbury E., 1891
8) *Guide to Traditional Customs of Britain*, Shuel B., 1985
9) *Derbyshire Well Dressings*, Caiger S L., 1947

Wirksworth

Spring bank holiday Monday (old Whitsuntide Monday)

Originally held on the Wednesday of Whit Week.

This old town, the one-time centre of the lead mining industry, relied on water carried in barrels on the backs of donkeys for their supply taken from springs in the water ground near Breamfield. The piping of this water from the same water ground took place in 1827 and terminated at taps. This is therefore a tap dressing, except that the locations of the taps are now forgotten. Today the dressings are at convenient places in the centre of the town; the churchyard railings, the cruck beam house, the old Health Centre, the chapel, etc.

There can be as many as fourteen dressings on display, some of which are by children from the local primary schools. These children we hope will be the dressers of tomorrow. Other organisations taking part are such as the Rotary Club, Methodist Church and various charities. One dressing which set a high standard is alas no longer with us, the Gate House Well. The wonderful thing about this latter team is that they did not belong to any shared body. They would meet every year as if by magic, dress their well to a very high standard, then disperse until the following year. It failed after many years of producing fine dressings.

Natural materials only are permitted, the glass eye introduced by a dresser was soon removed and cast aside.

The great boast by the Wirksworth dressers is that any well dressing is open house – anyone can call and watch the dressers, to ask questions and take part if they wish.

The clay for these wells is dug out of a bed of decomposed volcanic ash found in a local quarry. Years ago suitable clay was fetched from Denby Pottery, some ten miles away. Due to a lack of blue petals at this time of year, a nurseryman near Spalding in Lincolnshire force grows some blue hydrangeas for the purpose.

Encouraging young people to take part and learn is a strong factor in this town, for they are looked upon as tomorrow's dressers and most of them do so. The long evening of the Friday night prior to the Saturday when the wells are erected can go on into the early hours. The town fish fryer remains open until the last dressing is completed. It is this time when most of the dressers visit each other to comment, criticise and admire the competition. However, there is no competition as such, the judging of dressings and the award of prizes has been abandoned for many years so as not to disadvantage the wells dressed by the less well off.

A map showing the locations of the wells is produced and handed out to the visitors over the weekend. A well queen is chosen from the local young women who can boast a gown designed and made by Janet Reger, who donated it. She was a one-time resident in Wirksworth and had a factory here. The queen processes round the wells when being blessed, headed by the BMW Brass band – not the German motor car but the Brassington, Middleton and Wirksworth Band.

This page: Detail of the Gate House Well, 2000

Opposite page: Well by the church railings, 2000

In 1891, Bradbury said:

"Well dressings elsewhere (from Tissington) in Derbyshire have degenerated into a Saturnalia of Aunt Sallies and shooting galleries. Drinking fountains are decorated to give an excuse for a holiday. Special trains bring thousands of excursionists to the Wirksworth "tap" dressings each Whit-Wednesday. After partaking freely of the "tap", the trippers invade the Via Gellia Valley, and because the Lilies of the Valley are "not out" revenge themselves by tearing up the roots."

This valley was famous for its wild Lilies of the Valley, alas there are none to be seen today, now we know the reason why! This must be one of the first accounts of the effects of mass tourism on the Peak District. It was only a few years ago that trains ceased from delivering visitors to the Wirksworth dressings from Derby. There was a time when special trains were laid on from Sheffield and farther afield. The visitors still arrive in droves in special buses, cars and on motor cycles. Their presence is a mixed blessing as drunken rowdyism is not unknown.

An endowment of £100 was left by a Susan Marsden, the interest from which was to be used as prize money for the best dressed wells. The prizes were for the best adults' and children's wells. A set of rules for the judges was drawn up and used until recent times. This competition was abandoned.

Gate House

Whilst this is no longer dressed, it is hoped that it may be revived in the near future. This was placed to the right of the gate to the Gate House, at the end of the Causeway. The Gate House was once a property owned by the Gells of Hopton and once occupied by the estranged wife of Sir Richard Arkwright. An old yew tree provides a back drop for the board when erected. One of the authors was privileged to work on this dressing including trowelling the clay.

The dressers employed a different semi-professional artist each year to design the dressing. This led to a high standard of work, for the design is central to the finished work.

One of the team used to be the statistician, who kept a record of the time taken and the materials used. The result was put on display with the dressing when in situ. The statistics for the 1992 dressing were:

3,400 bits of maize and 1,200 coffee beans

5 buckets of moss, parsley and spurge

Hydrangea and pansy petals

Mahonia, laurel and copper beech leaves

Millet, hemp, linseed, poppy and sunflower seeds

Assorted stems of bark, peel and cones

Odd things like seaweed, shavings and egg shells

Japanese knot weed, Kiwi fruit and honesty pods

The collections at the well in 1992 amounted to £480 which was distributed to the Guide Dogs for the Blind, Save the Children Fund and Derby Children's Hospital.

Also located with this dressing was a small one by the Church of England Infants School.

Old Health Centre

In the yard to the centre on St John Street and dressed by the Rotary Club of Wirksworth. This is customarily of a simple design but most effective for that.

Methodist Chapel

To the side of the chapel in the yard facing Wood Street. Obviously this is always on a biblical theme. The space is shared with the County Infants School.

Market Place

Scouts and Guides

St. Mary's Churchyard and railings

Christian Aid
Alderwasley Hall School

Cruck Beam Cottage

Pre-school Play Group
County Junior School

Memorial Gardens

Senior citizens

Don Hughes who has his own chapter, number six, was a leading light at the Gate House Well.

Die, Dröme, France

Die is twinned with Wirksworth and during a visit of the French to England considerable interest was shown in the well dressings. As a result a small team from Wirksworth went to Die in 1996, and with the local people shared in dressing a well. This was undertaken to coincide with an annual ritual at Die when the sheep, some 4,000 of them, are herded along the main street to their summer pasturage in the mountains. Each of the four classes of the Chatillom Primary School undertook its own dressing.

Due to the high humidity, the seeds used soon sprouted.

Market Place Well, Wirksworth

Wirksworth Heritage Centre

The Heritage Centre in China Yard off the Market Place has a display of how a dressing is undertaken. As this was to be permanent a new approach was necessary.

Instead of clay, mastic as used on the Lindow frame (chapter six) was used. Crêpe paper was used for petals with great effect along with customary bark and seeds.

The mastic gave off oil which the bark and seeds absorbed. The whole dressing is painted with cooking oil from time to time to maintain its freshness.

The occasional slug attacks the seeds.

Youlgreave

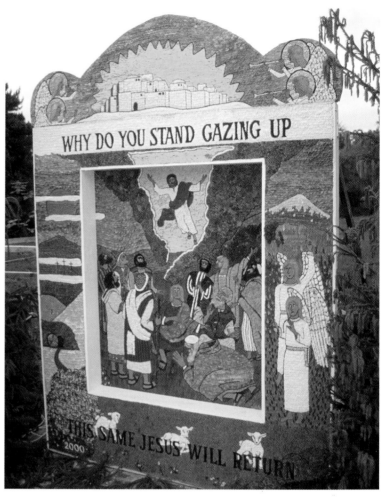

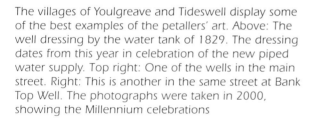

The villages of Youlgreave and Tideswell display some of the best examples of the petallers' art. Above: The well dressing by the water tank of 1829. The dressing dates from this year in celebration of the new piped water supply. Top right: One of the wells in the main street. Right: This is another in the same street at Bank Top Well. The photographs were taken in 2000, showing the Millennium celebrations

Opposite Page: A superb dressing at Tideswell, where the well usually displays a church, cathedral, etc

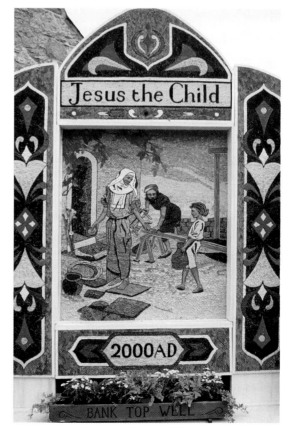

AD 2000

THE CATHEDRAL CHURCH OF S. ANDREW, WELLS.

THOU CROWNEST THE YEAR WITH THY GOODNESS

THOU VISITEST THE EARTH AND WATEREST IT

Youlgreave (or Youlgrave)

Saturday nearest to St John's Day, 24 June.

The dressings in Youlgreave are similar to those at Wirksworth as these also commemorate the piping of water to the village in 1829. This was originally piped to a stone tank, called The Fountain, which still exists and is dressed. Later the scheme was extended to five other, original taps. This system has now been extended to every house, shop, inn, etc. and the taps are now dry. The original water source was from a spring on a nearby hill but due to pollution water is now taken from Mawstone Mine – a disused lead mine. (1)

Dressing lapsed about 1850 to restart in 1969 when the water scheme was extended to provide extra taps along the main road through the village. The present dressings date from 1894.

The present dressings were enhanced by the influence of a Margaret Fell who introduced new ideas and techniques in the 1950s. Hers was a return to her village after a spell away. (2)

Youlgreave is unique in that it has its own private water company, every dweller is a share holder. The charges for water are significantly less than those charged to nearby villagers by the water authority.

These dressings cause controversy amongst purists, for at Youlgreave, they build up certain features such as hands and faces to give a hint at a 3D effect. It is similar to stump work. This certainly adds to the interest of the dressings and critics should remember that the dressings undertaken in the county are an invention not 200 years old.

In 1998 a dressing from Youlgreave along with six from other nearby villages were exhibited at the Chatsworth Country Fair, a prestigious event held annually at Chatsworth, the seat of the Duke of Devonshire.

In 1982, Youlgreave dressers were invited to Darmstadt near Frankfurt, Germany to undertake two dressings and Jim Shimwell with his wife demonstated a dressing at Hatfield House, Hertfordshire, the seat of the Marquess of Salisbury. (3)

A photograph of 1914 shows the local Lodge of Oddfellows in attendance with the village silver band at a well dressing. The photograph shows ribbons festooning the dressing. The theme was "How available are our dwellings." (4)

Frank Wilson, another family of dressers, when asked what it was like years ago, stated, "In my father's day not a buttercup was plucked until a giant 36 gallon barrel of beer was tapped. I'm not sure if well dressing was better in those days, but it was certainly more fun." (5)

In the year 2000, two Youlgreave stalwarts of the art of well dressing retired after spending many years designing and dressing wells in the village. Fred Shimwell – a legend amongst well dressers – and Margaret Fell both retired after 50 years of hard work. Also annoucing his retirement was Norman Wilson OBE, after 34 years as the chairman of the Well Dressing Committee. (6)

Sources:

1) Pers. com. Norman Wilson

2) ibid

3) ibid

4) The Bugle 2000 Ed: Emma Youatt

5) *Derbyshire Now!* The Big Feature. "Dressed to thrill" Amanda Volley, no date

6) Matlock Mercury 29 June 2000

Tideswell

Saturday nearest St John the Baptist's Day, 24 June.

Restarted shortly after the Second World War, they have set strong standards for artistry and quality. They specialise in detailed architectural dressings, whether new churches or old cathedrals, which are created each year in convincing detail.

The main dressing located on the Green has been transported elsewhere to display for charitable purposes. In 1946, a dressing was taken to Westminster Abbey to celebrate the 900th Anniversary of its foundation. (1)

In 1953, thirteen Tideswell men, supervised by Oliver Shimwell (Head Teacher at the village Church of England School), made a dressing for the Westminster Abbey Appeal Fund. This dressing was taken to Manchester where a short service was held in the centre of the city in the afternoon. It was relocated overnight to Dean's Yard, Westminster Abbey, where a short service was held, conducted by Dr Adam Cox, Archdeacon of the Abbey and treasurer of the fund. (2)

Oliver Shimwell is of a family famous for their skills in designing and making well dressings. Oliver once boasted that, "I have been well dressing for 35 years and my father before did it for 50 years." His son Edwin, 16 years of age at the time, was one of the team who worked at Dean's Yard. (3)

The famous "Ebbing and Flowing well", in a private garden at Craven House was dressed in the 1820s, celebrating the piping of taps from two springs on Sherwood Road; this lapsed in the 1860s. (4)

These dressings were originally started about 1820 with a lapse in the 1860s and the Second World War, restarting in 1946 after the hostilities stopped.

1) Notes and Queries No. 23 Derbyshire Advertiser 27 August 1953
2) *Well Dressing in Derbyshire,* Christian, R, 1987
3) ibid
4) ibid

A rear view of a dressing at Tideswell. Some boards need substantial support due to their size and weight

St Winifride's Well, Holywell –
the last official holy well site we
still have in use in Gt Britain

Two photographs of St Seiriol's Well, near Beaumaris, Anglesey. This is a Rag Well, but the 'rags' have recently been removed. Note the coins in the well and a bunch of flowers inserted into a crevice in the left hand wall. (P Naylor)

St Boniface's Well, Black Isle, Near Inverness, Scotland (E MacAskill)

Clootie in Cornwall, Cloutie in Scotland being pronounced clooty as in booty in the local vernaculars. They are also called rag wells in some parts.

Clootie or Cloutie are old terms for a piece of cloth. "Ne'er cast a clout till May be out" may not refer to shedding clothes too soon in Spring but to casting them at a holy well in May, the prescribed time for doing this.

The original and truly traditional well dressings were nearly always at holy wells and were certainly a Celtic practice. Traditions die hard in the Celtic fringes as there are wells still visited for their healing powers. These are found in Scotland, Wales, Cornwall and Ireland. They are frequently named after some minor saint, just take a look at a road map of Cornwall and see how many villages are named after saints.

Tracking down wells is not easy as people are somewhat secretive about them. The wells are dressed at all times at the whim of the visitor leaving votive offerings to the water sprites in the form of rags, called clooties in Cornwall and clouties in Scotland, clooties being pieces of cloth, although all sorts of offerings have been made, such as plastic bags, hats, etc. The theory behind this is that, if you remove a piece of clothing from the area of one's body that is a cause of pain or discomfort and leave it as a votive offering to the water sprite (or the saint of more recent time), a cure will ensue. Tradition has it that as the clooties rot away thus the condition in the pilgrim will fade away also. There is therefore a certain reluctance to clean these sites up for, if anyone should be foolish enough to remove a clootie, that person will inherit the condition. Therefore at certain clootie wells, the offerings hang flapping on the trees for years until they become nasty with the effects of weather and age.

There are some rituals to be observed for a stronger blessing, such as walking round the well a certain number of times and dropping votive offerings into the water. Dropping pins into the well was a favourite practice still in evidence in Derbyshire until as recent as the 1940s. Sometimes the pins have to be bent. Other offerings are sometimes made in the form of coins or anything precious. (1)

When Conventa's Well at Carrowbaugh, Northumberland was excavated, 14,000 or more coins, bronze figures, jewelry, glass, pots and a human skull were found. (2)

The Celts held springs in high regard, for it was the milk of mother earth issuing from a spring. The whiter the water the better as in the many Whitwells to be found. The cloudiness would be because of entrained air or the richness of the minerals contained in it. To avoid confusion some housewives in Ireland call tea towels clooties.

As each of these wells has its own story, a few are given below.

Cornwall

St Madron's Well, (Madern, Maddern, et al)

St Madron who died circa 545 AD was a Cornish hermit who, as legend would have it, lived by the well that carries his name. However, he was particularly active in Brittany. His feast day is on 17th May.

A local bishop recorded that in 1640 a John Trelille having close contractions of the sinews in his legs and having crawled on his hands and knees for 16 years, "upon three separate admonitions in his dreams, washing in St Madern's well and sleeping afterwards in what was called St Madern's bed was suddenly and perfectly cured". The bed referred to is a rock "seat" near to the well. (3) This took place over the first three Thursdays in May when he bathed in the waters. (4)

A Dr Borlase, writing in the 19th century and referring to a century before, records:

"To this miraculous fountain, the uneasy, the impatient, the fearful, the jealous, and the supersti-
tious, resort to learn their future destiny from the unconscious water. By dropping pins or pebbles
into the fountain, by shaking the ground around the spring, or by continuing to raise bubbles
from the bottom, on certain lucky days, and when the moon is in a particular stage of increase or
decrease, the secrets of the well are presumed to be extorted."

Bishop Hall of the local diocese bore witness of the efficacy of this well. (5)

Chapel Euny Holy Well

This chapel does now appear to be dedicated to a saint, unusual for Cornwall.

Years ago it was supposedly efficacious in the treatment for "the drying of humours, the healing of wounds and the treatment of infantile mesenteric diseases". In 1912 children were brought to the well on the first three Wednesdays of May to be dipped three times in the water against its flow. To be certain of a cure this should take place an hour before noon. (6)

In 1862 the dipping in the water was part of the Festival of the Moon together with Helston Floral Day and Padstow Hobby Horse Day. (7)

Scotland

St Boniface's Well

This well may be dedicated to St Boniface Curitan – there are about ten Saints Boniface – who died in 660 AD and whose feast day is 14th March. He was probably a Roman by birth but became Bishop of Ross after evangelizing the Picts and the Scots. (8)(9)

It appears as a spout on the road side on the A832 where people park dangerously to view it.

This must be the most used cloutie well in the British Isles. It would appear that everyone who pauses here feels compelled to make a votive offering whether they feel well or not (no pun intended). There is a huge collection of rags, pieces of cloth of every description, plastic bags, match boxes, you name it. It has been witnessed that a man took his shirt off, tore a strip off it and tied it to a tree branch. It is not recorded what he did with the rest of his shirt.

As the clouties seem never to be removed, although one year apparently the local authority did clean the site up, the clouties rot slowly, become dirty and end up looking a disgusting mess. The more clouties left the more people's curiosity, most of whom have no idea what it all means.

Many tourist buses stop here to allow the passengers to " take part in an old Scottish custom". The irony is that the "well" is a modern pipe inserted into the hillside – the actual well discharges lower down onto the nearby beach. (10) If you should chance to visit the site, car parking is restricted to the roadside verge by which people drive their vehicles at some speed. This could end up no longer as a healing well but one for road accidents.

Wales

St Seiriol's Well

Little is known about this saint except that he was a Welsh monk and hermit after whom Puffin Island is named – Ynys Seiriol – off the coast of Anglesey. He died in the 6th century and his feast day is 1st February. It is located close to an old Priory Church, still in use.

Newlyweds used to race from the church to this well and the first to arrive would be the one to wear the trousers throughout the marriage. (11)

Ireland

St Kevins's Well

Known in Ireland as St Coemgen supposedly born at the foot of the White Fountain in Leinster of royal descent. Baptized by St Cronan, he was ordained becoming a hermit in the valley of the Two Lakes in Glendalough. Seven years later he went to Disert-Coemgen as a solitary, founding a monastery there. He undertook a pilgrimage to Rome. His friend was St Kieran of Clonmacnois who raised the son of King Colman of Ui Faelain. It is said that he was 120 years old on his death. (12)

St Columkille's Well

Born circa 521 AD at Gartan, Donegal of royal descent. Having studied at Leinster and Clonard, he was ordained circa 543 AD, from when he founded the monasteries of Derry, Durrow and Kells. After killing 3,000 warriors in a battle he did penance by converting the same number of pagans to Christianity. We next find him at Iona in 563 AD where he built a monastery, spending his time converting the Picts of Scotland including King Brude at Inverness. He was responsible for monks being sent out

One off Well Dressings (see page 92)

The J. R. R. Tolkien dressings, Beren and Luthian; Below: The dressings at the Tolkien grave, Oxford

The dressings for
the Derbyshire
Japan Festival,
1991. "YOUKOSO"
means welcome

all over Europe becoming a major influence in the Celtic church until the arrival of St Benedict and the emergence of the Roman practices. He died on 9th June 597 AD which date became his feast date. (13)

Doon Well

This well is overlooked by Doon Hill the traditional location where the O'Donnell chieftains were inaugurated, the last time being in 1603 when Niall Garbh O'Donnell was so proclaimed. The rags here are attached to a Hazel Tree.(14)

Tobar Isa

This originates from the 7th century and is maintained by the Cahir Development Association. The soldiers from the Kilcommon Barracks used to visit this well to pray for protection prior to active service. Visitors attach rags to what is known here as the Rag Tree. (15)

Clootie type wells elsewhere.

Armenia   Rags tied to trees as votive offerings but without a well (16)
Greece & Cyprus   Rags tied to trees (17)
Tuva, Central Asia (18)

St Winifride's Well, Holywell, Flintshire, North Wales.

This chapter cannot be complete without a mention of the only official holy well site we have still in use. A visit to this well is worth the time as the spring issues into a large stone lined bath in the open air, there are smaller baths under the cover of a chapel. Many people have sought and received cures here and not so long ago they left their sticks and crutches behind to prove the point. This latter tradition has been banned of late.

Whilst this well does not attract or encourage votive offerings such as clouties, it is recommended as a must to the well enthusiast as a remnant from when such places were numerous and attracted many meaningful people.

It is in the village of Holywell on the A5026 which is off the Chester to North Wales road, the A55. Cars can be parked on the road outside.

A mixture of legend and fact describe the founding of this well. Apparently on 22nd June, 660 AD, Winifride – et. var. and also known as Gwenfrewi – refused the advances of a local chieftain, Caradoc. In his rage the chieftain cut her head off. A spring rose at the spot where her head fell and later Winifride's uncle Beuno restored it and her life was restored to her. Some time later she became a nun at Gwytherin, Denbighshire where fifteen years after her miraculous recovery she became the Abbess. Her feast day is 3rd November. (19)

1) *Ancient Wells and Springs of Derbyshire*, Naylor P J., Cromford, 1983

2) *Sacred Wells Holy Wells*, in Parabola, the Magazine of Myth and Legend, Freeman M., Spring 1995

3) ibid.

4) Fentynyow Kernow. *In search of Cornwall's Holy Wells*, Straffon C., 1998

5) *Gentleman's Magazine* from www.antipope.org/feorag/wells/hope/cornwall.html

6) *Chapel Euny Holy Well* from www.st.just.online.freeuk/ceuny-well.htm

7) ibid.

8) www.bath.ac.uk

9) www.saints.catholic/boniface.html

10) In Litt. Eileen MacAskill of the Inverness Field Club

11) www.saints.catholic/seirial.html

12) www.saints.catholic/kevin.html

13) www.saints.catholic/columkille.html

14) www.geocities.com/Athens/trog/7080/
   doonwell.Html

15) www.tipp.ie/wishoingw.html

16) website.lineone.net/~geoff.burton/wells/
   wells.html

17) In Litt. Williams R., Matlock

18) website.line one.net/-geoff.burton/wells/
   wells.html

19) www.saints.catholic.org/saints/winifred.html

Above & top right: (detail): the Festival of Work-shops and Schools, 1993. Right: Royal Horticultural Society flower show, Hampton Court Palace, 1996, having a Derbyshire theme.

Petalling the word "anniversary",
Hand's Well, Tissington

Above: Petalling well boards at the former stables, Tissington Hall

Below: At Marston Montgomery village hall

This method is average for Derbyshire and applies generally across the whole spectrum of well flowering. It is based on the experiences of one of the authors who for many years was a volunteer with the Gate House Well, Wirksworth, Derbyshire.

Dressing a well in the now traditional fashion, that is by petalling, demands both hard work and infinite patience.

There are nine basic requirements in the order of use:

1) a location for the finished board
2) a team of volunteers
3) a suitable board
4) clay and salt
5) a theme with a design
6) petalling
7) transport and erecting
8) volunteers to oversee the dressing
9) volunteers to take it down

1) Location

The site of a well, spring or tap is desirable but not essential. The public are now aware that the locations are of lesser importance to the design and execution of the board. Favourite places are churchyards, school yards, village greens, road sides (although one should consider the safety aspects of so doing!), people's front gardens, the public house yard, etc. Seek and obtain the permission of the land owner first for they will be exposed to public gaze for a few days.

2) Team of volunteers

People must be chosen who will stay the course. If they are new to the craft, they must accept the possibility of long hours particularly on the night before the well is moved and erected. They will suffer backache, headache, clay on their clothes, suffer criticism when they do it wrongly, acceptance that the designer's opinion is the only one that matters, and enjoy euphoria experienced when the well is erected in its temporary resting place. There is no experience quite like it and the writer (PN) has seen many a grown man cry at this point.

3) Suitable board

This has to be made to suit the constraints of the site. A decision must be made whether or not it is to be in one piece or a triptych. Remember the bigger the board the more it will weigh and these when loaded with wet clay can be very heavy. It is not unknown for a JCB to be brought in to move the board when finished.

The board base should be of timber planks, say 150 mm x 10 mm and pine is ideal. The planks should be supported on a timber frame, ledger and braced if necessary. The edges of the board should be provided with lipping in hard wood such that it is nailed to the frame but stands proud about 40 mm. The whole thing must be well assembled so as to take the strain of the weight of the clay. The board must have a matrix of galvanized clout nails having large heads. These should be nailed in such that the heads are 25 mm proud of the board and for safety's sake the pointed ends of the nails should not protrude beyond the rear of the board. If they do they must be ground flush. Wire netting is sometimes used as reinforcement for the clay.

If the board is to be a triptych, consideration must be given as to how you intend to join the whole thing together in its resting place. Consideration should also be given as to how you intend to stand the thing such that it does not fall onto the admiring public, particularly when the wind is blowing a gale. Is the site level? Can the assembly be tied back? It really does pay to involve a carpenter!

4) Clay and salt

Prepare the boards by soaking them such that they do not take up any water from the clay. Methods vary from immersion in a stream or pond for several days to playing a hose onto them for a few hours. Remember that the boards at this stage will float, so if they are placed in a stream tether them to a tree. It must be demoralizing to see them float away.

You will need clay. This must be of the correct consistency, of sufficient quantity and free. Sources of clay have been traditionally: dug out of the ground, clay way boards in quarries, potter's clay (not cheap if you have to buy it). The clay when moist must have a "sticky" feel to it. It must be free from stones and pebbles.

It will need digging out from wherever you find it and transported to your frames. Strong plastic bags holding as much as a person can carry should be used. The amount you need is to measure the volume of the boards. Fill a bucket with clay and weigh it and calculate its volume, the clay is so heavy that you can ignore the weight of the bucket. From this a calculation can be made of the amount of clay required to fill the frames and the number of bucketsfull to a bag. But add 10% for drying out and other factors.

Place the clay in a suitable receptacle for puddling. The old fashioned tin bath is fine. Add cooking salt in the ratio of a generous handfull to a bucket of clay. Spread the salt as evenly with the clay as possible, this is used as a retardant to drying out. Wearing gum boots (or bare feet if you feel adventurous) "walk" the clay by pumping your feet up and down such that the clay is moved and mixed. Remove any stray stones and pebbles which always seem to be present. This is leg aching work and it pays to have a relay of puddlers. Stop puddling when the clay has a smooth plastic consistency. If it is dry add a little water at a time to achieve the correct plasticity.

The boards should be placed horizontally on trestles and stabilized by packing them. If you are using a church hall, or something equally sensitive, cover the floors with polythene sheets to protect them.

The next job is equally laborious. Empty the bags of clay onto the boards by a few bags at a time. This should then be spread over the boards such that it is level with the wooden lipped edges and well placed behind the nail heads. A smooth and level finish is necessary.

Be careful to clean up properly, spare clay can get everywhere and is difficult to remove from moss! Having said this, it is essential that some spare clay is available for repairs.

5) Theme and design

If you have access to a professional artist all the better.

The design has to be based on a specific theme with a text if so desired. Traditionally this has been biblical but there is an increase in secular subjects. One village features churches and cathedrals for instance.

Having decided on the theme it is advisable to engage a professional artist or graphic designer. Many an amateur village artist has produced excellent designs. The person chosen should be in charge of the petallers' choice of materials used. If the artist is a newcomer to the art required, it would be advisable that he/she view good designs by others. He or she should be aware of the finished drawing and the message of the design which should be similar to glazed church windows.

Initially the design should be produced on small sized paper, say A3 or A4, and coloured as a guide to the appearance of the finished well. If more than one board is used for the dressing and if the design spans these boards, the artist's presentation should echo this.

After the team has approved the design and after any constructive comments have been taken on board, the design needs to be transferred on to large pieces of grease proofed paper exactly the same size as the actual dressing, a separate piece for each board when there are more than one. The outlines need to be marked with indelible marker.

Finally, the design has to be transferred onto the clay by laying the design papers onto it. If the frames have pointed or rounded tops ensure that the design is the correct way up. Pat it onto the clay gently to secure the papers from moving. Prick through the paper using wooden cocktail sticks to leave holes in the clay at every line junction and at intervals of 100 mm between. Gently roll the papers off and lay to one side. The final task is to join the holes up to replicate the design. This can be done by running a cocktail stick along the clay to join the holes up. One dressing uses wool laid onto the clay and there are no doubt other methods yet to be found.

Left: Children at work on the Norbury Well, near Ashbourne, which is dressed by school children, 1995. The girls are Rachael Wheeler (left) and Charlotte Ratcliff

Below: Close-up of Marston Montgomery's main board, 2000

6) Petalling

This activity is time consuming and exacting and must be done properly for the dressing to succeed.

Whilst the clay and the boards are being prepared, volunteers should be out and about collecting materials for the actual dressing. The time of the year will dictate what is available in the garden and in the countryside. Any flower will suffice and there are favourites such as spurge, hydrangea, (see appendix, p 95). Mosses are very useful as is thin bark which lifts off trees without disturbing the living bark underneath. The "cones" from alder trees can be very useful but not cones from conifers unless green. Another favourite are rhubarb "seeds" which are actually the flower buds. Resort is made to prepared and shop bought seeds such as millet, maize and coffee beans. The material used must be "natural" whatever that means, some construing it to mean vegetable matter that has actually grown. This is a contentious point amongst certain dressers who would frown on the use of coffee beans and would be horrified if coal were suggested. This latter material seems attractive when the dressing is held in a coal mining community. Most dressers would agree that pebbles and sea shells are inappropriate albeit the latter have grown.

The timing of the dressing will dictate what flowers are available naturally from the countryside and some resort to buying them from florists and supermarkets. Hydrangeas have been known to be forced to provide petals out of their season. One dressing, now defunct, collected potted hydrangeas from Spalding, Lincolnshire and after stripping the flowers off them sold the potted roots to visitors at the well to defray their cost.

The first job is to reinforce the lines in the clay with edging material and this is where maize and coffee beans come in useful. Seek out the maize seeds which are flat and fix them into the edge of the clay. Press the coffee beans into the clay firmly and they will stay there.

Always collect petalled flowers complete with some stalk and store until use in jars of water to keep them fresh.

Petalling should be undertaken with great care – they must not fall off, wash off in rain and retain their colours. Remove the petal from its stalk and press the heel of the petal into the clay by pushing the heel into the clay with an instrument, a cocktail stick is useful here. Lay the petals as you would fix roof tiles (some people refer to this as tiling), by lapping them down from the top of the board towards the bottom to create a water shed.

Carefully sprinkle small seeds onto the areas desired and press them onto the clay with a small flat surface, a small plastic box for example.

Decide who will do which area to avoid conflict and overlap. If the material used looks "wrong" remove it and try something else, this is where you would need to repair the clay. Should the clay show signs of drying use a mist spray to wet it gently but avoid puddles. If in doubt about your choice of material seek advice from the artist or, in his/her absence, a dresser present with much experience.

The boards must be finished in time for their removal and erection and this might mean working late on the night before. Indeed the last night is often a time of frenetic activity with a prize offered to the dresser who guesses the time of completion. At a well in Wirksworth the prize was the golden chip award, a bag of chips from the local fish and shop which remains open on this night until all the dressings are finished.

For the newcomer, many mistakes will be made and patience lost, but the final dressing is worth all the agony and heartache.

7) Transport and erecting

If the dressing is not undertaken on site, the boards will have to be moved and erected at the agreed location. Visit the site the night before and ensure that nothing can block the location and access to it. Enrol the assistance of the police beforehand if necessary. They will usually oblige by coning off the area.

Clear the space around the boards, the last thing you wish for is something to fall over when you are moving a finished board which can weigh up to 750 kg. You will need a team of strong people. Hoist the board gently onto its base such that it is vertical. Do not be alarmed by the noise! This will be from the loose seeds as they rattle down the board and onto the floor. Clear the trestles out of the way.

If the distance to the location is small the boards can be carried there. If the location is some distance away transport must be used. The board can be laid across a pick-up truck or trailer and transported at a slow speed with the helpers walking at the sides ready to shout if the boards start to slip or any other calamity.

The erection of the boards is pure engineering, and the job is finished. For the first time, the petallers will see the finished dressing and all your fears for its appearance will evaporate at this truly great and emotional time.

Return to the place of dressing and clean it up and leave it as you found it.

8) Volunteers to watch over the dressing

The collection boxes should be laid out daily and taken in at night. The volunteer must be willing to answer questions about the dressing, how it was done, how long it took, how many people worked on it, and so on. The volunteer will also have to tell parents that their little darling should neither pull the petals off nor try to scoop the clay out.

An unfortunate aspect of well dressing which has arrived over the last thirty years or so is vandalism. It is heartbreaking to return to the dressing on the second day of its life to find that someone has damaged the clay by kicking the dressing or by using it for target practice with stones. The police are powerless at times like this for they have insufficient constables to allow the dressings to be guarded overnight. The decision has to be made whether or not to guard it using volunteers – a heavy commitment. The damage due to vandalism at Etwall in the dressings of the year 2000 was so bad that a reward of £100 was offered by the Etwall Well Dressing Association for information leading to an arrest.

As the days progress so does the deterioration of the dressing. Certain petals have fugitive colours and these show signs of bleaching. As the clay dries out it starts to crack, particularly when the wind is blowing. To partly counter the latter a mist spray should be used to keep it fresh. This is why some villages take their dressings down after only three days or so. Most leave them up for 6-8 days and towards the end the dressings are looking very sad indeed.

9) Volunteers to take it down

At the end of its display the dressing must be taken down. The easiest way is to break the clay out and collect it on the spot. Make certain that there is no clay left behind the nail heads and netting when used. On the assumption that you will repeat this the following year, you will need someone's unused outhouse, barn, etc in which to store it. Check the bolts and grease them and pack it all away safely.

Start to plan next year's dressing. The pleasant way to do this is to hold a soirée at one of the dressers' houses. A subscription can be made to defray the cost or each attendee can contribute something. It is a pleasant round off for well dressing week, when you can congratulate each other and look forward to another time together.

Remember to take the phone numbers of all those willing to return, appoint a co-ordinator as a contact point and send the collected money off to your chosen charities. For those who reuse the clay each year there is the added problem of collection and storage of it.

Points to remember:

a) Book well in advance the locations for both the act of dressing and the location for the finished dressing.
b) Be careful of others' property when dressing under cover and leave it as you found it. If you have agreed a rent for the use of the premises remember to pay it.
c) Respect the petallers and their foibles, they are volunteers and deserve respect.
d) Remember to pay the charities.
e) Do have a soirée for the helpers.
f) Remember to arrange the blessing with the church.
g) Get your blessing included in lists published by local Tourist Information Offices.
h) Involve your local newspaper.
i) Before choosing a date talk to the police and check to see if a nearby community are also dressing a well at the same time. This latter could be either an advantage or a disadvantage, only local knowledge can decide.
j) If your dressing is a success, people will return the next time.

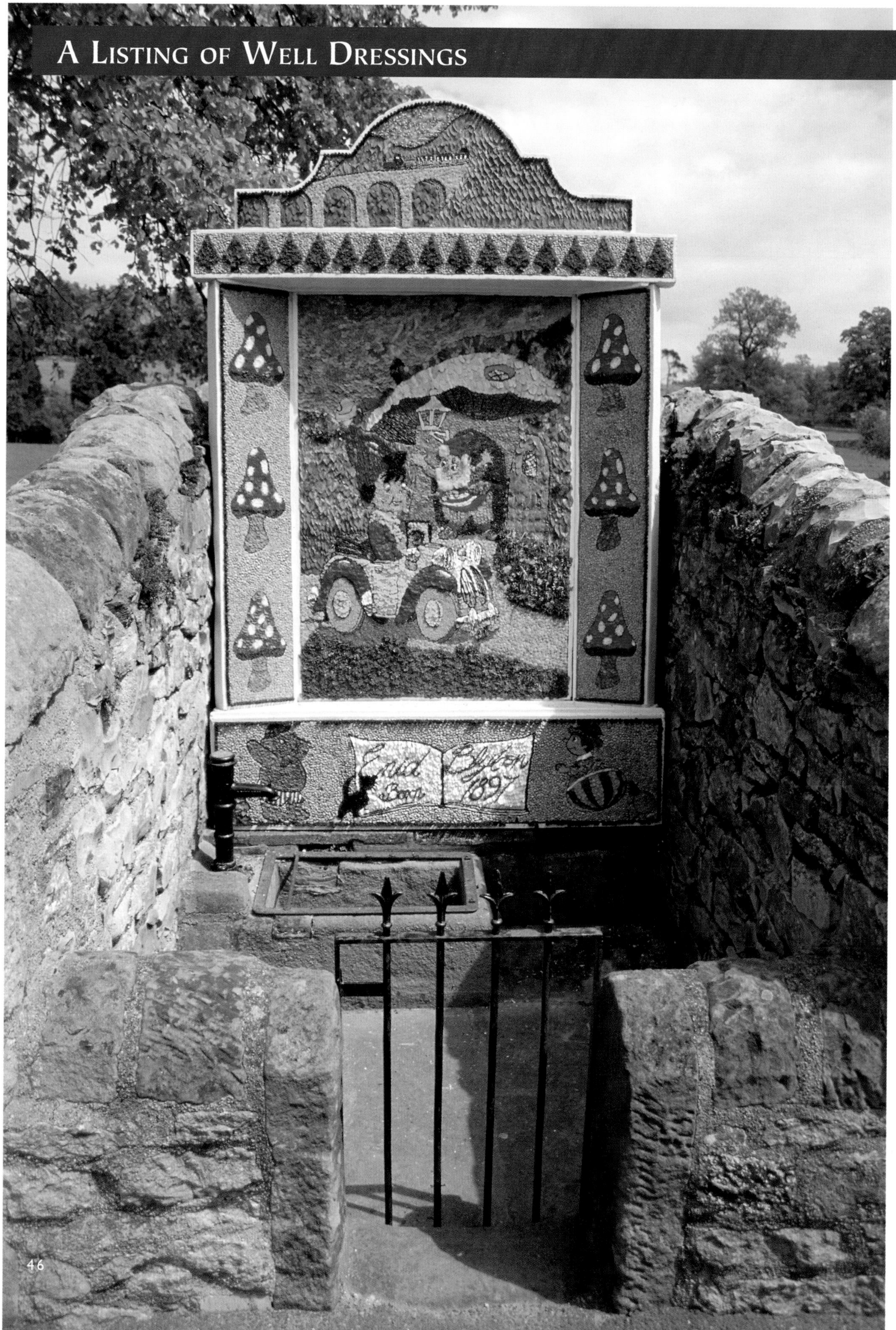
Enid Blyton
Born

The authors have endeavoured to make this a definitive list of existing and lapsed dressings. It is probably the most complete list known to date, but the situation is always shifting, a few wells fail and there are new dressings every year.

The list is by county in England with Cornwall, Wales, Scotland and Ireland as separate areas. Within these areas the lists are alphabetical by city, town and village. The counties are not in alphabetical order, it starts with the most populous county for well dressings, Derbyshire. The counties then radiate away from Derbyshire as the incidence appears to decrease the further one gets from this county.

The wells are usually blessed on the day they are erected except that they would be more likely to be blessed on a Sunday if the dressing is erected on the Saturday, the day before. All dates are taken from the 2001 dressings. Anyone intending to visit a well dressing should first check with the local information offices for the exact date and time of the blessing if needed. They should also be able to advise you if the dressing will take place. For example in the year 2001, certain dressings had to be cancelled because of the restrictions enforced due to the foot and mouth disease outbreak.

Beware of popular dressings, as a car parking problem may exist, so arrive early if you can. The dressings are quieter on a weekday, but be aware that the dressings deteriorate with the passing of the days so do not leave it too long. They are left on public display for varying periods generally from 3 to 8 days. After three days they start to look a little shabby and the clay having dried out starts to crack and craze, this can be accelerated if there has been a wind blowing onto the dressing.

The word well is used throughout and this implies springs, taps or nothing at all other than a frame. Some dressings are called frames and the finished dressing is sometimes called a petalling with a single instance called flowering.

Most villages have a well dressing committee which organises the events.

The totals of villages undertaking dressed wells for England only was found to be as the list below, county by county:

County	Active Villages Dressing 2001	Lapsed	Actual Dressings 2001
Derbyshire	89	49	200
Nottinghamshire	3	8	3
Staffordshire	5	6	13
South Yorkshire	5	2	5
Greater Manchester & Cheshire	6	-	6
North Yorkshire	1	-	1
Gloucestershire	1	-	1
Lincolnshire	-	1	-
Somerset	-	1	-
Totals:	110	67	229

Clootie, Cloutie and Rag Wells have not been included.

The total of 229 wells dressed (200 in Derbyshire) represents a huge amount of work for many people in one season. If 200 person hours is ascribed as an average for each dressing, a grand total of 45,800 person hours which at 40 hours per week would equate to 22 years!

Certain of the dressings are referred to as "now lapsed". This is believed to be the case at the time of writing, and the authors apologise if any of these dressings prove to be active. Obtaining up to date information has not been easy. The dates, may vary, sometimes by weeks in many cases.

The dates given are bassed on information available for 2002 in most cases.

Opposite page: Greaves Lane Well, Ashford-in-the-Water, 1997, celebrating the birth of Enid Blyton

DERBYSHIRE

Alfreton - now lapsed.

Allestree - now lapsed.

Ashford-in-the-Water
Between Buxton and Bakewell off the A6T.
Erected on the last Saturday in May and blessed the following day.
Up to six wells dressed.
Revived in 1930 and 1954.
Coincides with their flower festival at the Holy Trinity church and a sheep washing demonstration at the Sheepwash Bridge on the Saturday.
Demonstrations available.

Ashover - lapsed but now joined with Brackenfield.

Aston-on-Trent
Off the A50 south of Derby.
Erected on the first Saturday of July and blessed on the same day.
One well dressed.

Ault Hucknall (with Glapwell and Rowthorne).
Off the Chesterfield to Mansfield road, the A617.
Erected on the third Saturday of July and blessed the same day.
Have been known to use sheet silver, oyster grit, sheep's wool and dog hair.
One well in each village.

Bakewell
On the Buxton to Matlock road, the A6T.
Erected on the last Saturday of June and blessed on the day after.
Started early in the 18th century to coincide with an attempt by Bakewell to become a spa village. These lapsed along with the demise of hydropathy in Bakewell to be revived in 1971.
Up to four wells dressed:
>   Bath Gardens, 1st Boy Scouts
>   Bath Gardens, Garden of Remembrance
>   Butter Market, King Street, Bakewell Mencap Carers
>   Church Alley, South Church Street, in the graveyard, by the Explorers (new in 2000)
All are dressed in the same location without friction.
Coincides with their carnival, with a Carnival Queen.
Two dressings from here were exhibited at the Chelsea Flower Show, 1977.

Bamford
On the Hathersage to Glossop road, the A6013, just south of the Lady Bower dam.
Erected on the second Saturday of July and blessed on the following day.
One well dressed.
Started 1991.
Coincides with their carnival week with a band, shows, displays, stalls, etc.

Barlborough
On the Chesterfield to Worksop road, the A619, and adjacent to Junction 30 of the M1.
Erected on the third Friday of July and blessed the same day.
One well dressed.
Started 1875.
Coincides with the flower festival in St James' church.

Barlow
North west of Chesterfield on the A6051.
Erected on the Wednesday after 10 August (St Lawrence's Day) and blessed on the same day.

Three wells dressed.

Tradition has it that that these dressings began as a thanks offering for the village's delivery from the great drought of 1615, also referred to under Tissington in Chapter Two.

Started in 1840 and lapsed to be revived in 1890 when the Duke of Rutland had built a well house for the use of the villagers and from this date without a break, including two world wars. However it is claimed that the dressings date back to the time of Queen Elizabeth I. The well house was given to the village in 1920.

This dressing has to be undertaken in situ due to the size and the weight of the four boards which fill the well arch. Wilfred Needham worked on this dressing for 60 years following his father.

They use only wild flowers, scorning garden plants altogether.

Coincides with their flower festival in St Lawrence's Church. Also a carnival and craft fair.

Demonstration available.

Baslow
On the Bakewell to Chesterfield road, the A619.
Erected on the first Saturday of July and blessed the day following.
Two wells dressed. Started 1984.

Belper
On the road from Derby to Matlock, the A6T.
Erected on the second Saturday of July and blessed on the day following.
Up to twelve wells dressed during their well dressing festival.
Held in the Belper River Gardens.
Demonstration available in the River Gardens.

First well dressing dates from 1838 when the Mill Lane Well was dressed and in the following year four wells were dressed. The present dressings are a 1986 revival after having lapsed for World War II.

In the days when the mills were in full production the Wakes week was a great event which involved the whole town and attracted visitors from afar, special trains being laid on from Sheffield and Derby. In 1889, prizes totalling £50 were available for the tap dressings and street decoration. In this year, the dressing on the Butts took first prize of £8 with £2 added as it had been in previous years. No mean sum this, it would be the equivalent of £100 today. The second prize of £5 was won by the dressing on the Market Place and the one at Bridge Foot came third with a prize of £3. The fourth prize went to a dressing at the Duke of Devonshire inn, it is not recorded if this exhibitor won anything.

A photograph (below) of 1880 shows the dressing at the Butts, with all the male dressers (note no women). This dressing is of interest as it does not depict a scene or quotation from the Bible, as was the custom at this time. It is fairly plain with much woodwork and side panels with finials. The motto on the top arch is "Welcome to all" (aka well come to all?). The foreground is of rough stones and foliage.

Bakewell, 1997 and 2000.
Above and top right: Bath Gardens; Middle right: Detail from the Bath House Well in 2000; Bottom right: The well outside the Butter Market in King Street, 1997

Opposite page: Four wells at Ashford-in-the-Water, 1997. Top left: Little Well, Greaves Lane; Top right: Great Batch Well, Church Street; Bottom left: Sheepwash Well; Bottom right: Detail from Greaves Lane Well

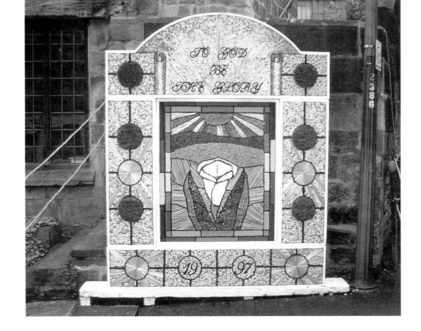

In 1876, in the evening of 5 July, a member of the "Old Model Prize Band" from Sutton in Ashfield, Nottinghamshire, which had been playing at the tap dressings fell off the brake which was transporting the band home. He died instantly, he was 38 years of age. This happened at the toll bar at South Normanton.

Birchover - now lapsed.

Bolsover
On the Chesterfield to Ollerton road, the A632.
Erected on the third Saturday of July and blessed on the same day.
One well dressed.
Demonstration available in Bolsover Castle.

Bonsall
Off the Cromford to Newhaven road, the A5012.
Erected on the last Wednesday of July and blessed the same day.
Four wells dressed.
Coincides with their Carnival week.
   The dressings began in 1927, organised by Fred Bunting the local Primary School Head Teacher and Miah Doxey the owner of a local fish and chip shop.

Brackenfield
Between Matlock and Clay Cross.
Erected on the Saturday of the May Spring Bank Holiday weekend and blessed the same day.
Since 1984.
Up to five wells dressed:
         Main Board
         Methodist
         Millennium (new in 2000) on a re-opened well on the village green.
         Ashover School
         Stretton and Handley School
Demonstrations are available in the Church Hall.
Coincides with their Flower Festival at the Methodist Church with an exhibition in the Village Hall.

Bradbourne - now lapsed.

Bradley - now lapsed.
Near to Ashbourne.
A dressing was recorded here in 1839.

Bradwell
On the B6049 south of Castleton.
Erected on the Saturday before the first Saturday of August and blessed on the day following.
Since 1949 but some say that dressings took place in the early 1900s.
There are four dressings as follows:
         Townend Well
         Church Street Well – this dressing is dangerously close to a busy road
         Smalldale Well
         Children's Well
Coincides with their carnival and gala on the Beggars Plot Playing Field.
This coincides with the Small Dale Wakes when they have a Gala Queen and Princesses.
   These dressings are unusual in that they keep the clay moist by allowing the design paper to stay in position and by cutting out with a razor blade when they are to be dressed.
   They buy twelve boxes of hydrangea from the Trelissick Gardens, by the King Harry Ferry, near Falmouth, Cornwall (A National Trust property).
Demonstration available.

Breaston - now lapsed.

Brimington
North of Chesterfield on the A619 off the A61 Chesterfield to Sheffield road.
Erected on the second Sunday of July and blessed the same day.
One well dressed.

Buxton
On the road from Manchester to Bakewell, the A6T.
Erected on the first Sunday of July and blessed the same day.
Since 1840 spasmodically but regularly since 1923.
Four wells dressed:
 St Anne's Well, The Crescent
 Market Place
 Children's Well, Spring Gardens
 Lion Head Fountain, Tourist Information Centre
Coincides with the Buxton Festival and Carnival with a Wells Queen.
Demonstration available, usually in the Paxton Suite, Pavilion Gardens.

The provision of a water supply and the subsequent dressing of wells in celebration at Youlgreave and Wirksworth was followed by Buxton in 1840. In this year, the Duke of Devonshire erected two 'Fountains' which were supplied with water from outside the village. One of these was in the Market Place which ended the days of carrying water uphill from Lower Buxton. In commemoration, the fountains, were dressed along with floral decorations around the village. There were morris-dancers, bands, foot races and a greasy pole, all attracting the attention of people from the surrounding villages.

The day of the well dressing became the busiest day of the year. Fortunately, a good description of the event was published which enables us to appreciate the proceedings and atmosphere reasonably well (Book of Days, Chambers, R, Vol 1 1862-4):

"Vehicles of all kinds, and sadly overloaded, pour in at an early hour: the streets are filled with admiring groups and bands of music parade the town. The crescent walks are planted with small firs and the pinnacles of the bath-house have each a little flag – alternately pink, white, blue and yellow – the effect of which is extremely good, connected as they are by festoons of laurel. But the grand centres of attraction are the two wells. On an occasion when we visited the place, that of St Anne's was arched over; the whole groundwork covered with flowers stuck into plaster, and on a ground of buttercups were inscribed, in red daisies, the words 'Life, Love, Liberty and Truth'. Ferns and rockwork were gracefully arranged at the foot, and amidst them a swan made of the white rocket, extremely well modelled; an oak branch supported two pretty white doves, and pillars wreathed with rhododendrons completed the design, which was on the whole very pretty. We can scarcely say so much for the well in the higher town, which was a most ambitious attempt to depict 'Samson slaying the lion,' in ferns, mosses, fir cones, bluebells, buttercups, peonies and daisies – a structure twenty feet high, the foreground being occupied with miniature fountains, rockwork and grass. Much pains had been lavished upon it; but the success was not great.
The morris-dancers form an interesting part of the day's amusements. Formerly they were little girls dressed in white muslin; but as this was considered objectionable, they have been replaced by young men gaily decorated with ribbons, who come dancing down the hill, and when they reach the pole in the centre of the crescent fasten the long ribbons to it, and in mystic evolutions plait them into a variety of forms, as they execute what is called the Ribbon Dance. In the meantime the children are deligating themselves in the shows, of which there are abundance, the men at the entrance of each clashing their cymbals and proclaiming the superiority of their own in particular – whether it be a dwarf or a giant, a lion or a serpent; and the merry-go-rounds and swing-boats find plenty of customers. Altogether, it must be allowed that there is a genial and kindly influence in the well-flowering which we should be sorry to see abolished in these days, when holidays, and the right use of them, is a question occupying so many minds."

The article included an illustration of St Anne's Well, which is reproduced on page 1.
In 1863, the London & North Western railway line opened its new Buxton Station. A few days later between 20,000 – 30,000 people arrived for the well dressings. It must have come as quite a jolt to those who had grown up in the comparative tranquillity of the 'old' Buxton that had enjoyed village status.

Buxworth

The Tower of Babel

Opposite page: The Market Place Well dressing,
Buxton, in 2000, surrounded by the fair

Left: St Anne's Well, Buxton, 2000;
Bottom left: Church St. Well, Bradwell, 1985;
Bottom right: Bamford, 2000

Erected on the first Saturday of July and blessed on the day following.
One well dressed.
Located in the Canal Basin.
Organised by the Buxworth Well Dressing committee now incorporating the Association of Buxworth and Clayton and Buxworth School, in association with the Chapel-en-le-Frith dressings. A well dressing workshop is held on the second day for teaching newcomers the art. This is held in the Buxworth memorial Club (the Buggy Club).

This dressing was undertaken for the first time in the millennium year, 2000. The theme was the "Railway Children" by Edith E Nesbit who had relatives nearby. The scene taken from the book was of a railway cutting. The well chosen for this dressing was German's Well, originally named after German Wheatcroft the one time wharfinger here, a member of the Wheatcroft family of Cromford where they were the wharfingers also. The water for the spring emanates from two sources: a natural spring and a sough from the now defunct Moseley Hall Colliery. The idea for this dressing was from the landlady at the local Navigation Inn, Lynda Hall. Forty people helped with the work, with donations from local benefactors, mostly companies and parish councils. Also materials were donated: timber from Dorma, 90% of the flowers came from the local Safeway Supermarket at Chapel-en-le-Frith, with cash from PVC Limited.

The people connected with this dressing are to be congratulated for their entrepreneurship, vigour and tenacity. In one year that have established a tradition at Buxsworth with a web page and heavy involvement of the local public house.

Calow - now lapsed.

Calver Sough - now lapsed.

Chapel-en-le-Frith
Off the Manchester to Buxton road, the A6T.
Erected on the first Saturday of July, the week of the feast day of St Thomas Becket and blessed on the day following.
Since 1995 for most but the Warmbrook School Well has been dressed since 1982.
Six plus one wells dressed:
>   Town Well: Amenity Society at the Old Brewery Well
>   Children's Well: Warmbrook School
>   Nanny's Well – a medicinal spring
>   Windy Wall Well, Bowden Lane West – an old drovers' well
>   Bowden Lane Well, also an old drovers' well
>   Bear Well – where a performing bear used to be watered
>   Buxworth Well see under Buxworth
Demonstration available.

Chatsworth – a demonstration board usually features at the Chatsworth Country Fair held on 31 August and 1 September.

Chelmorton
Off the B5270 south of Buxton.
Erected on the Saturday nearest to St John the Baptist's feast day, 24 June, and blessed the same day.
Since 1990.
One only well dressed and located by the small stream "The Illy Will Water".
Coincides with their flower festival at the church.
Demonstration available.

Chesterfield
Erected on the first Saturday of September and blessed on the same day.
Four dressings.
Started 1991 (revival).
Demonstrations available in the Tourist Information Centre, Peacock Centre Courtyard, Low Pavement.

Clay Cross

On the Chesterfield to Alfreton road, the A61.
No details available.

Clowne
Off the A618, M1 Junction 30 to Edwinstowe road.
Caiger mentions a dressing here in 1947.
Clowne's Heritage Community School won the first prize for the well dressing here in the Greenwatch scheme with a prize of £500.

Coal Aston
On the B6056 off the A61 Chesterfield to Sheffield road.
Erected on the first Saturday of July and blessed the same day.
One well dressed.
Coincides with their village gala and flower festival in the Wesleyan Reform Church.
Dressing is located in the yard of a Public House.
See Dronfield.

Codnor - now lapsed.

Cowley Mission - see Holmesfield.

Cressbrook, Monsal Dale
North of the Buxton to Bakewell road off the A6T.
Erected on the second Sunday of June and blessed on the same day.
Coincides with their Gala Day.
Up to two wells are dressed on the village green.

Cresswell - now lapsed but see Elmton.

Crich - now lapsed.

Cromford - now lapsed.

Cutthorpe
North west of Chesterfield off the B6051.
Erected on the third Friday of July and blessed on the same day.
Up to three wells dressed.
Revived in 1978 after a gap of 30 years.
The pre World War II dressings had no religious themes.
Coincides with gala week.
Demonstration available in situ.

Dale Abbey
South of the road from Derby to Ilkeston, the A6096.
Erected on the first Monday of May and blessed the same day.
Two wells dressed.

Darley Dale - now lapsed.

Derby
   Market Place - Erected on the second Monday of June and blessed the following Saturday.
   One well only outside the Tourist Information Centre.
   Demonstration available in the Guildhall Theatre, Market Place.

   Chester Green - Erected on the Saturday prior to Spring Bank Holiday weekend in late May and blessed the same day.
   Since 1982.
      One well is dressed with up to two boards near to the site of two Roman wells which provided Derventio with its water. These Wells were outside the walls of this fortified Roman garrison.

   St Alkmund's Well - Bath Street

Opposite page; Top left: Chapel-en-le-Frith, 1998; Top right: Cressbrook, 1997, with Poppy Marsden (LP's grand daughter); Bottom left: Close-up of the Chelmorton Well (bottom right) note the use of cut rhubarb stems, 2000 (see also page 83)

Above: Elmton, 2000
Right: The Children's Well, Eyam, 2000;
Bottom left: Great Longstone, 2000;
Bottom right: Little Longstone, 2000

Not dressed for some years. This well was a place of pilgrimage for Northumbrians as was St Alkmund's Tomb in the now lost St Alkmund's church. His sarcophagus is in Derby Museum. It was said that the lid of his tomb was worn smooth by the knapsacks of the pilgrims. St Alkmund was killed in battle and his body was brought from Lilleshall in Shropshire to Derby and was laid by the well until a shrine had been built.

This well was dressed from 1870 for fifty years and revived again recently and abandoned again.

Landau Forte College - now lapsed.

Royal Crown Derby - now lapsed.

Doe Lea - now lapsed.

Dronfield
On the B6057 off the A61 Chesterfield to Sheffield road.
A "Dronfield Feast of Flowers" with festivals in sixteen churches in the area including well dressings at:
> Holmesfield – Cowley Mission Church
> Coal Aston – Wesleyan Reform Church
Starts on second Saturday in July.

Dronfield Woodhouse
West of Dronfield (see above).
Erected on the second Friday of July and blessed on the same day.
Only one well dressed.
Demonstrations available in the Methodist Chapel.

Duffield - now lapsed.

Earl Sterndale
South of Buxton off the road to Ashbourne, the A515.
Erected on the fourth Sunday of August and blessed on the same day.
One well dressed.
Coincides with their Flower Festival.
Demonstration available at Home Farm.

Eckington - now lapsed.

Elmton
Off the A616 south of Clowne.
Erected on the fourth Friday of June, and blessed on the same day.
Since 1985.
Three wells dressed:
> Village Well
> Elmton Children
> Cresswell Infant School.
Coincides with their Fayre held on the village green.
Demonstrations available in the Old School Room.

Elton
West of Winster off the B5056, Grangemill to Bakewell road.
Erected to coincide with the village fête in July.
Since 2000.
Located on an actual well in Well Street.

This single dressing is undertaken by the children of Elton C of E School, originally to celebrate the millennium with the title "Water of Life". However it looks set to be repeated annually under the direction of one of the teachers, Liz Parker.
The millennium dressing won several awards as follows:
> Derbyshire County Council – Greenwatch scheme gaining first prize for Primary schools of
> £800 for their section and the overall award, the Lafarge Redland Special prize of £500.

Peak District National Park – for achievement in the park first prize for schools and the overall winner.

Astonishing for a first time dressing especially one by children.

Etwall
Between Derby and Uttoxeter off the A516.
Erected third Saturday in May and blessed on the same day.

Since 1970 to mark the centenary of the village school. This was undertaken by the teachers and the Women's Institute who dressed Etta's Well with help and advice from Tissington and Youlgreave.

Up to eight wells dressed including the original Eatta's Well which is a spring fed from an underground stream from the old hospital in Sandypits Lane, under the chip shop, and Main Street to the edge of the Green near to the church. This spring has never been known to run dry.

> Town Head Well – Etwall Women's Institute
> St Helen's Well – residents and friends of Mill Meadow Way
> Church Well – 1st and 3rd Etwall Guides
> Scout Hut Well, Sandypits Lane – 1st and 5th Derby Scout Group
> Primary School Well – parents and staff of Etwall Primary School
> George VI Playing Field Well – residents of Etwall village
> Frank Wickham Hall Well – 1st and 3rd Etwall Brownies
> Hawk and Buckle Inn – at the inn well

All except the Town Well are located on actual known wells.

It is believed that the boards used for the Town Head Well are the biggest in the county.

Demonstrations are available on the village green.

Eyam
On the B6521 off the Chapel-en-le-Frith road, the A623.
Saturday prior to the last Sunday (Plague Sunday) in August and blessed the following day.
Revived 1951.
Three wells dressed:

> Townhead Well
> Town End Well
> Children's Well

These dressings commemorate the 1665-6 visitation of the Black Death which killed 257 villagers, about a third of the population. A service is held in Cucklet Delf (private land). Clarence Daniel, the late local historian, wrote two hymns for the occasion, one for adults and the other for children.

A carnival queen is chosen and crowned during the well dressing service.

Demonstrations available.

Findern - now lapsed.

Foolow
Off the Chapel-en-le-Frith road, the A623.
Erected on the Saturday prior to the last Sunday of August and blessed the same day.
Two wells dressed on the village green.
Started 1983.
Coincides with their Village Wakes and Fayre.

Furness Vale - now lapsed.

Glapwell (see Ault Hucknall).

Glossop (see Tintwhistle).

Great Hucklow
Off the B6049 off the Chapel-en-le-Frith road, the A623.
Erected second Thursday of August and blessed the same day.
Up to two wells dressed.

Great Longstone

Off the A6020 which is off the road from Bakewell to Buxton .
Erected on the second Saturday of July and blessed the same day.
One well dressed by the school.
There is a fête Queen with attendants and a Church Fête held on the Longstone School grounds.
The actual work of dressing can be viewed in the school.

Grindleford - now lapsed.

Handley (see Brackenfield).

Hardwick - now lapsed.

Hartington
On the B5054 off the Ashbourne to Buxton road, the A515.
Erected on the second Saturday of September and blessed on the same day, Wakes Saturday.
Two wells dressed on the Green by the Mere near to the old village pump.
Started 1980.
The two wells are:
      Main Well – Chapel driveway
      Children's Well – corner of School Lane
Coincides with their Wakes Week.

Hathersage
On the Sheffield to Castleton road, the A6187.
Erected on the first Saturday of July and blessed the day following.
Up to two wells dressed.
Started in 1996.

Heage
South of the Ambergate (A6T) to Ripley road, the A61.
No details available.
Started in 1986 by Peter Davies of Belper who led the team at Belper.

Heanor - now lapsed.

Heath
On the Chesterfield to Mansfield road, the A617, close to Junction 29 of the M1.
Erected on the third Saturday of July and blessed on the same day.
Since 1975.
One well dressed.
This dressing used to coincide with Ault Hucknall.
Tom Price (manager of adult education in the area) started this dressing inspired by those at Bonsall.
Coincides with their flower festival in All Saints church.

Higham - now lapsed.

Holbrook - now lapsed.

Holmesfield
West of Dronfield.
Erected on the second Friday of July and blessed on the same day.
One Children's Well on Main Road.
Coincides with their celebrations week comprising a flower festival with private gardens open to the public.
Demonstrations available in situ.

Opposite page; Top left: Eyam, 2000; Top right: Hartington, 1990;
Bottom left: Foolow, 2000; Bottom right: Children's Well, Foolow, 2000

Cowley Mission Church.
Erected on the second Saturday of July and blessed on the same day.
One well dressed.
Coincides with their Flower Festival, see Dronfield.

Holmwood - now lapsed.

Holymoorside
South of the Chesterfield to Baslow road, the A619.
Erected on the Thursday prior to August Bank Holiday and blessed on the same day.
Two wells dressed:
>   Main "Whistling" Well
>   Children's "Penny" Well
Coincides with their gala.
Restarted in 1976 after an interval of about 80 years.
Whole flower heads are used hence they refer to it as flowering rather than petalling. All flowers are from local gardens and none are bought.
Demonstrations available in situ.

Hope
On the Castleton to Hathersage road, the A6187.
Erected on the first Saturday nearest to 24 June and blessed on the day following.
Three wells dressed.
A 1949 revival.
Hope prefers cultivated flowers.
There is a Wells Queen with a band, displays, etc.
Coincides with their carnival and Wakes Week held on the Hope Sports Field.
Demonstrations available in Losehill Hall.

Ilkeston - now lapsed.

Kniveton
Between Ashbourne and Wirksworth on the B5035.
Erected on the Saturday nearest to 24 June and blessed the day following.
Dressings here were recorded for 1894.

Little Longstone
Located as for Great Longstone.
Erected on the second Saturday of July and blessed on the day following.
One well dressed.

Litton
South of the Chapel-en-le-Frith to Baslow road, the A623.
Erected on the Saturday nearest to Midsummer's day 24 June, and blessed on the Sunday following.
Since 1969.
One well dressed at Litton Primary School.
Originally aided by Oliver Shimwell to commemorate the centenary of the village school.
Demonstration available in village hall and school.

Makeney - now lapsed.
Caiger refers to this being dressed in 1947.

Mapperley - now lapsed.

Marston Montgomery
West of the Ashbourne to Uttoxeter Road, the A515.
Erected on the second Sunday in June and blessed on the same day.
Up to two wells dressed.
A revival since 1987 which commemorated the 50th anniversary of the building of the village hall, where they are dressed.

Up to two wells are dressed near to the church.

The Victorian well was closed due to the seepage of polluted water from the churchyard. In 1901 the village bus shelter was erected and this became the location of the well dressing. The second dressing is by the school children and is displayed at the school entrance.

Photographs in the village hall recall dressings in 1906 and 1910, the tradition here being a century old at least. On 3rd July 1908 a well was dressed for the annual festival of the local Oddfellows' Lodge.

The millennium dressings commemorated, amongst other things, the restoration of the church bells, which were pealed after the blessing of the dressings. Attractions were laid on with stalls and games and Osmaston Wind Band.

Demonstration available in the Coronation Hall.

This village had the rare distinction of having its initials being the same as the millennium date as follows: Marston Montgomery = MM = 2000.

Matlock
On the road from Bakewell to Derby, the A6T.
The chalybeate sough at the bottom of Allen's Hill, sometimes known as the Allen Hill Spa, at the Dimple, used to be dressed sporadically but not for five years now. Doreen (Tottie) Holden undertook the first recorded dressing in June, 1978, having no previous knowledge or experience. The dressing was undertaken by the All Saints Brownie pack. They used a board made redundant by the Wirksworth County Junior School. The theme was the Brownie motto "Lend a Hand", showing children helping an old lady. Alas the dressing was vandalised on the first night after erection.

Morton - now lapsed.

Middleton-by-Youlgreave
West from the A6T at Haddon Hall (Pickory Corner).
Erected on the Saturday prior to Spring Bank Holiday weekend in late May and blessed the following Saturday.
Since 1977 to commemorate the Queen's Silver Jubilee.
A village market was held with local, national and international events.
Two small boards of arrows, dressed by children, were placed at the roadside to guide visitors to the events.
One well dressed.
Demonstration available in situ.

Milford
South of Belper on the A6T.
Erected on the Saturday after May Day and blessed on the same day.

Millthorpe
West of Dronfield.
Erected on the first Saturday of July and blessed the same day.
One well dressed.
A 1979 revival after lapsing before World War II.
The dressers use the techniques from the Barlow wells, whose dressers taught the Millthorpe people.
Demonstration available outside the Royal Oak Inn.

Monsal Dale (see Cressbrook).

Monyash
East of the Ashbourne to Buxton road, A515.
Erected on the Saturday prior to Spring Bank Holiday in May and blessed the same day.
Since 1974.
Up to five wells including two boards by children.
The Newton Well was the first to be dressed in 1974 with help from Litton.
Demonstrations are available in Quaker Chapel.

Left: Litton, 2000;
Above: Children's Well, Litton, 2000;
Bottom Left: Detail of Litton well (above);
Bottom right: Marston Montgomery, 2000

Top right & left: The two Monyash Wells, 1997. The above board is placed on the car park which is on the site of one of the village's four meres; Top left: Norbury Well, 1997; Below: Matlock, 1978

Norbury
To the west of the Ashbourne to Uttoxeter road, the B5033.
Erected on the first Friday of July and blessed on the same day.
Only one well dressed by and at Norbury Primary School.

Ockbrook
On the B5010 off the Derby to Nottingham road, the A52.
Erected on the third Saturday of June and blessed the same day.
This is undertaken by the Moravian Community and is within their grounds.

Old Whittington
North of Chesterfield off the Sheffield road, the A61.
Erected on the Friday nearest to Midsummer, 24th June, and blessed on the same day.
Only one well dressed.
Coincides with their Gala held on the Mary Swanwick School Playing fields and flower festival held in St Bartholomew's church.

Openwoodgate - now lapsed.

Osmaston
Near Ashbourne - now lapsed.

Over Haddon
South of the B5055 from Bakewell.
Erected on the Saturday prior to Late Spring Bank Holiday in May.
Two wells.

Palterton
Off Junction 29 of the M1.
Erected on the third Saturday of June and blessed on the same day.
One only well dressed.
Coincides with their flower festival at St Luke's mission church.

Peak Forest
On the Chapel-en-le-Frith to Baslow road, the A623.
Erected on the first Wednesday of July and blessed on the same day.
Up to two wells dressed.
First recorded in 1904 and revived in 1994 at the instigation of the Comptroller of Chatsworth, James Fisher.
Coincides with the Rose Queen Fête on the Recreation ground.
Demonstration available in Billy's Barn.

Pilsley
Off the Chesterfield to Bakewell road, the A619.
Erected on the second Thursday of July and blessed on the same day.
Up to four wells dressed on the village green.
Revived 1968.
Coincides with the village fair which has a Queen with a band, games, etc..
Demonstrations available in the Smithy Yard.

Quarndon - now lapsed.

Riber
Turn south off the Matlock to Alfreton road at Tansley, the A615.
Erected on the second Saturday of July.
One well dressed.

Ripley
Erected third Saturday of June and blessed on the following day.
One well only dressed.

Demonstration available in the Tourist Information Centre.

Roston - now lapsed.
Frith gives an evocative account of a dressing of about 1900. "The Roston Well – it bears the name of Friday Well – stands in a farmyard at the back of a little Primitive Methodist Chapel, and I found the entrance decked with branches and boughs of trees, with rustic arch adorned with cheap flags, large festoons of laburnum and of lilac, and a scroll bearing the text 'O ye wells, Bless ye the LORD, Praise Him and magnify Him forever'. Over the well itself an elaborate structure had been raised which had evidently kept the good women of Roston very busy for the previous day or two. A large wooden frame had been made, rounded at the top and divided into separate partitions. In the centre was a representation of Battle Abbey, with the outline of the building picked out in haricot beans. A Union Jack waved above it – the red supplied by geranium petals, the blue by cornflowers, and the white of rice. The background was of moss and other green stuff. Devices were formed out of Indian corn, linseed and small fir cones, daisies in intersecting rings and as borders were a feature of the decoration, and bright colours were obtained from the different flower petals. "Peace unto All" was the legend at the top of the frame, and at the foot "God save the King", while a dove of haricot beans spread benign and sheltering wings over all. The whole was a most creditable display of ingenuity and good taste. The frames are coated over with wet clay into which salt has been kneaded in order to keep it moist and adhesive, and the flowers and other ornaments are then stuck on one by one."

Today's well dresser would recognise all of this over one hundred years later.

Rowsley
On the Bakewell to Matlock road, the A6T.
Erected on the last Saturday of June and blessed the following day.
Since 1974 when the horse trough outside the Peacock Hotel was dressed to commemorate the centenary of Cauldwells Mill, with help from Jim Shimwell of Youlgreave. This established a partnership between the mill and the village.
Up to three wells dressed.
Coincides with their Festival and Gala and a Flower Festival in St Katherine's church. They crown a festival princess.

Rowthorne (see Ault Hucknall).

Sandiacre - now lapsed.

Scarcliffe (Bolsover).
Erected on the third Thursday in June and blessed the same day.

Shirebrook
Near Bolsover.
Erected on the last Friday in June and blessed the same day.
Coincides with their flower festival held at the Holy Trinity church.
One only well dressed.

South Normanton - now lapsed.

South Wingfield - now lapsed.

Spondon
On the A6096 off the Derby to Nottingham road, the A52.
Erected on May Day Bank Holiday Monday and blessed the same day.
One dressing at the St Werburgh's House Nursing Home.
Demonstrations can be seen prior.

Stainsby Mill, Hardwick Hall - now lapsed.

Stanton-by-Dale - now lapsed.

Peace Well, off Hollow Lane, Mayfield, 1997

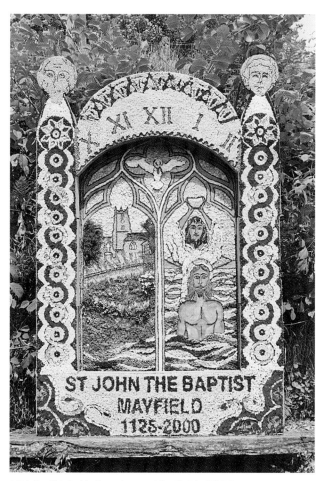

Middle Well, Hollow Lane, Mayfield, 2000

Peace Well, off Hollow Lane, Mayfield, 1996

Middle Well, Hollow Lane, Mayfield, 1999

Left & above: The two Rowsley Wells, 2000. The well above is opposite the Peacock Hotel and the one to the left is erected on the other side of the A6; Bottom left: Mayfield, 1896; Bottom right: Main Well, Stoney Middleton, 2000

Starkholmes
On the back road from Matlock Green to Cromford Bridge.
Erected on the fourth Saturday of June and blessed the day following.
A gala Queen with a parade and entertainment are all held for this dressing.

Stoney Middleton
On the Baslow to Chapel-en-le-Frith road, the A623.
Erected on the Saturday (usually the third) after the end of school summer term in July and blessed the same day.
Up to three wells dressed in the Nook:
> Main Well
> Children's Well
> Bath Garden Well

The Main Well is a real well, the other two are springs.
   The Bath Garden Well is adjacent to the Bath House built by Lord Denman a local resident in 1815 for the local work people to use for bathing. Legend has it that this site was used by the Romans for bathing. The other dressings are in the churchyard.
Revived 1936 and 1947 after being suspended due to World War II before which it started.
   The occasion is accompanied by a brass band, with teas and cakes for sale, various games and other events during the week. Oliver Shimwell of Youlgeave revived these dressings post World War II.
A special hymn was written by an ex-incumbent, the Reverend Alexander Fraser.
Demonstration available in the Moon Inn.

Stretton (see Brackenfield).

Sturton - now lapsed.
A dressing was recorded here in 1894.

Swanwick - now lapsed.

Taddington
Off the Buxton to Bakewell road, the A6T.
Erected on the third Saturday of August and blessed on the same day.
Two wells dressed one of which, High Well, is at an altitude of 400m above the village.
Started in 1990.
Demonstrations available, follow signs in the village.

Tansley
On the Matlock to Alfreton road, the A625.
Erected on the first Saturday of July and blessed on the same day.

Thorpe - now lapsed.

Tibshelf - now lapsed.

Tideswell
On the B6049 between the A6T and the A623.
Erected on the Saturday nearest to St John the Baptist's Day 24th June and blessed on the same day.
Since 1946 but lapsed in the 1820s and 1860s.
Up to four wells dressed.
Coincides with their Wakes Week, market (charter dated 1250) and Carnival day with parades (following Saturday).
Demonstrations available.
   Also a board is located in the church during their Flower Festival usually in the second full week of September, from the Sunday for a week. This festival is occasional and may not appear every year and possibly on different dates.
See chapter two concerning these dressings.

Tintwhistle
North of Glossop on the A628 Barnsley to Manchester road.

Erected on the fourth Friday in June and blessed on the same day.
One only well dressed by the Tintwhistle Women's Institute.
Located on Old Road known as the Holy Well, it has a reputation for helping to relieve the symptoms of arthritis and rheumatism. From 2000.

Tissington
Off the Ashbourne to Buxton road, A515.
Erected on Ascension Day, May.
Six wells are dressed including children's well.
Demonstrations available, see the signs in the village.
See pages 16-20 and 97-126 which describe the preparation process there.

Upper Langwith
Off the Bolsover to Ollerton road, the A632.
Erected on the second Thursday of July and blessed on the same day.
One well dressed.
Coincides with the flower festival in the Holy Cross church and the Village Fair.
Demonstration available.

Waingroves, Ripley.
Erected on the 2nd Saturday of May and blessed on the same day.
Demonstrations are available in the Methodist Church Hall.
From 1999.

Whaley Bridge
On the Manchester to Buxton road, the A6T.
Erected on the last Sunday of June and blessed on the same day.
One well is dressed and incorporates coal as a reminder of that industry, now gone, in the area.
From 2000.

Wardlow
On the B6465 off the road from Chapel-en-le-Frith to Baslow.
Erected on the last Tuesday of August and blessed the following Sunday.

Warslow - now lapsed.

Wessington
On the A615 between Matlock and Alfreton.
First Saturday in July. No details available.

West Hallam
West of Ilkeston off the A609.
Erected on the second Saturday of July and blessed on the same day.
Five wells dressed.
Started 1978.
Located:
        26 Beech Lane
        School Square
        Old School House, Beech Lane
        Old Post Office, Beech Lane
        The Punch Bowl public house

Westhouses - now lapsed.

Whitwell
Off the Chesterfield to Worksop road, the A619.
Erected on the second Saturday of July and blessed on the same day.
Four wells dressed by the Scout and Guide Group as follows:
        The Scouts
        The Guides

Top left: Coffin Well, 1998; Top middle: Town Well, 1998; Top right: Town Well

Right: High Well, Taddington, Fetching water from this location must have been a real chore; it is high above the village

Opposite page; Top left: Detail from the board in the church yard, Tideswell (main photograph), 2000; Top right: The Tideswell Brownies board also in 2000

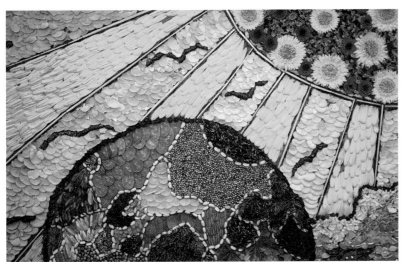

Venture Scouts

Leaders and committee

Started 1971, when the village pump was dressed.

Demonstration available in the Scout Headquarters.

Located:

The Square

Butt Hill

The Green (2)

Wirksworth

West of Cromford on the B5023.

Erected on the Saturday prior to Spring Bank Holiday weekend in late May and blessed on the following day.

This was originally a tap dressing to commemorate the provision of piped water to the town.

There can be up to 14 dressings which were originally tap dressings but they now occupy any useful space for demonstrating them.

This coincides with a carnival.

A well dressing Queen is crowned wearing a dress designed and made by Janet Reger, a one-time resident of the town.

Wirksworth Heritage Centre on Crown Yard off the Market Place has a permanent display about the well dressing.

See chapter two concerning these dressings.

Wormhill

Off the A6049 north of the Buxton to Bakewell road the A6T.

Erected on the fourth Saturday of August and blessed the same day.

Two wells dressed at the Brindley Well on the village green and in the churchyard. The Brindley well commemorates the life of James Brindley (1716-1772) the canal engineer who was born in Tunstead nearby. In one year, £1,400 was donated by visitors to this well, the money being used by the church and village hall. Oliver Shimwell is a designer here.

Started 1951.

Demonstrations available, follow the signs in the village.

Wyaston - now lapsed.

Two dressings were recorded here in 1860 known as the Edlaston Well and Wyaston Pump.

Youlgreave

West of the Bakewell to Matlock road A6T at Haddon Hall (Pickory Corner).

Erected the Saturday nearest Midsummer, 24th June, and blessed on the same day.

Since 1829 when piped water was laid to taps in the village for the first time. The 1849 dressings lapsed as did the 1894 dressings.

Five taps are dressed:

Coldwell

Reading Room (now Church Well)

Fountain – which is a stone tank on the village main street.

Holywell Lane

Bank Top

Demonstrations available in various garages in the area.

Also a dressing is often sited in the church during their Flower Festival held over August Bank Holiday weekend.

See chapter two concerning these dressings.

NOTTINGHAMSHIRE

Church Warsop - now lapsed.

Headon

North of the Worksop to Lincoln road, the A57, south of Retford.

The last Saturday in June blessed on the day following.

Dressed in 1981 the subject being the Church of St Peter, Headon and not again until the millennium year 2000, when the subject was "Farewell 1900s". It is not known when the next dressing will take place.

Sited on the Ladywell, named after the mother of Christ.

Kirkby in Ashfield - now lapsed.

Mansfield - now lapsed.

Newstead - now lapsed.

Pleasley
Off the Mansfield to Chesterfield road, the A617.
Erected on the second Saturday of July and blessed on the day following.
One well dressed.
Coincides with their flower festival in St Michael's church.
Demonstrations available.

Scarcliffe
South of the Chesterfield to Ollerton road, the A632.
The third Saturday in June and blessed the day before.

Skegby - now lapsed.

Stapleford - now lapsed.

Teversal - now lapsed.

Worksop - now lapsed.

STAFFORDSHIRE

In 1680 Dr Robert Plot visited Staffordshire prior to writing his History of Staffordshire, published in 1686. He stated that they had a custom in the county of adorning the wells with boughs and flowers. He observed the custom on Ascension Day at Brewood and Bilbrook. He made no mention of the current custom of pressing flowerheads or petals into soft clay. Plot went on to state that the custom was observed at all "Gospell-places, whether wells, trees or hills: which being now observed only for decency and custom sake, is innocent enough. Heretofore too it was usual to pay this respect to such wells as were eminent for curing distempers, on the Saints day whose name the well bore, diverting themselves with cakes and ale and a little musick and dancing; which, whilst within these bounds, was also an innocent recreation".

Brewood (pronounced Brood)
Lies south of the A5 near to M6, Junction 12.
Now lapsed.
Lot mentions a dressing here in 1680, comprising "boughs" of flowers.
Frith also mentioned them in 1905.

Burton-upon-Trent - now lapsed.
Held at the Bass Museum.

Endon
On the Leek to Stoke-on-Trent road, the A53.
Erected on the May Day (Spring Bank holiday) and blessed on the same day.
Two wells are dressed.
Demonstrations are available in Well Dressing Field.
  Started in 1845 to celebrate the piping of water to a trough in the village. This is therefore a tap dressing. On this occasion the local blacksmith, carpenter and tailor procured "home made pikelets

Three of the Millennium Wells
in Youlgreave

Opposite page; Above: Gate
House Well which also features
on page 22. together with the
original design; Bottom left: The
Scouts and Guides Well, 1997;
Bottom right: Wormhill, near
Buxton, 1953

soaked in butter, bread and butter, cured ham and other good things: a cup of tea and cream if desired and rum to celebrate the first dressing." The latter had occurred earlier in the day, the well being dressed with oak leaves, boughs and flowers.

The well was built by a Thomas Heaton.

In 1853, the Staffordshire Advertiser reported that at 2.00 pm:
> "A procession of villagers, headed by the village band went to the church for a service and then sung a hymn at the well. There followed tea in a marquee, after which there was country dancing, which was kept up until 1.00 am. Some 400 people attended the event."

It was about this time that Endon changed the method of dressing to flower petals set in clay on wooden frames as with the present day manner. By 1856, an organising committee had been established and one shilling (5p) was charged for tea and dancing. A quadrille band was engaged in 1861 and from 1964 Endon brass band provided the entertainment. Well dressing seems to have been firmly established as a popular event.

In 1865, a May Queen was chosen attended by twelve girls who danced around the maypole, wearing hats, white frocks with frills and sashes, six of the girls wearing their sashes in the boys' fashion. The tradition of a Queen of the wells lives on to today.

In 1872, the train from Leek was full and the afternoon train from Stoke-on-Trent was also full despite having double the number of carriages and also despite the pouring rain.

2,271 people visited the dressing in this year.

In 1916, the event moved from the Whit Weekend to the Spring Bank Holiday.

Today this is still a popular event in the North Staffordshire's calendar of events and attractions. The proceeds of the event were originally distributed to the poor. The beneficiaries now include the Sunday schools, youth groups and other voluntary organisations. (See photograph on page 82)

Grindon - now lapsed.
In 1900, Grindon advertised a well dressing in the Ashbourne News, details were not given.

Ilam - now lapsed.

Lichfield
Off the road from Birmingham to Burton-on-Trent and Derby, the A38.
Erected for Ascension Day.
One dressing at St Chad's Well located west of the church on the opposite side of a brook now culverted. This was once a place of pilgrimage but fell into disuse, but now fully restored. St Chad (Ceadda) brother of St Cedd, was educated under St Aidan on Lindisfarne. He died in 673 AD at Lichfield. His feast day is 2nd March.
Since 1995.
The dressing of 1999 was a precursor to a further dressing in 2000 to commemorate the millennium when a children's dressing was added, created by the pupils of Year 6 of St Chad's School. The main dressing was designed by the Mothers' Union.

Longnor
On the B5053 off the Buxton to Ashbourne road, the A515.
Erected on the last Saturday of August and blessed on the following day.
Two wells dressed.
Coincides with Longnor Races.
Demonstrations available on Church Street.

An unsuccessful attempt was made to establish well dressing but came to nought. This was an attempt to revive a previous practice. A further attempt in 1983 has been more successful and continues to today.

Mayfield
Off the Ashbourne to Uttoxeter road, the B5032 and close to Ashbourne, Derbyshire.
Erected the third Saturday in June and blessed on the same day.
Four wells are dressed:
    Trough Well

Peace Well
Middle Well
Children's Well
The Trough Well is at a drinking trough for animals, the remainder are wells.
Three wells were dressed in 1896 but this short lived attempt lasted only two years. At that time the dressings were located:
Hollow Lane
The lane from Mayfield Hall to the main road
Bentley Cottage garden
Demonstration available at the Old Hall Farm. (See photographs on page 70-71)

Newborough
On the B5234 west of the Uttoxeter to Lichfield road, the A515.
Erected first Monday in May and blessed on the same day.
Since 1978 but there is evidence of a dressing here from 100 years before.
Three wells dressed.
A demonstration is available prior in the "Hut", the Newborough Youth and Adult Centre.
A flower festival is held at the same time and a Maypole is demonstrated. They have a May Queen also.

Rudyard Lake - now lapsed.
The proprietor of the Rudyard Lake Hotel (now renamed Hotel Rudyard since 1886) by the name of Henry Platt started a well dressing in 1871 in an attempt to attract more customers to his hostelry. It seems to have survived until 1873.

Rushton - now lapsed.
A well dressing took place in 1867 at St Helen's Spring (or St Daniel's Spring) south of the village at Rushton Marsh. From 1897 the event was enhanced by a May Queen. The last dressing took place in 1933.

Tutbury - now lapsed.

SOUTH YORKSHIRE

Conisborough
On the A630 Rotherham to Doncaster road.
A well was dressed here for the Millennium 2000.

Dore
On the Sheffield to Baslow road, the A621.
This village was in Derbyshire until 1935.
Since 1959.
Erected on the first Saturday in July and blessed eight days later.
Two wells are dressed and located on the Village Green:
Village Green Well
Guide Well
Coincides with a Flower Festival at the church.
These dressers were inspired by those at Eyam.
Demonstrations available in the Scout Hut.

Harthill
East of the Rotherham to Clowne road, the A618.
Erected on the second Monday of July and blessed on the same day.
One well only dressed.
   They also dress the well with hangings of colourful fabrics and materials for Christmas and Easter. When dismantled the fabric is donated to charities. This is as close as you will get outside Scotland and Ireland to the original dressings using clouties.

Above: Endon, 1961; Right: St. Chad's Well, Lichfield, 2001

Above: Dore, 1996; Right middle: Bakewell, 1997;
Right bottom: Detail from the main Tideswell Well, 2000

Detail from well boards:
Top left: Tideswell
Top middle: Ashford-in-the-Water
Top right: Chelmorton, showing rhubarb stems

Left: Youlgreave, 2000. Here faces are traditionally made in clay and then painted with natural substances
Below: Middleton-by-Youlgreave, 1997

Norton
South of Sheffield on the A61
When: No details available.
Since 1972.
One dressing.
Norton was a village in Derbyshire until 1935.
The horse trough is used and Clarence Daniels hymns are sung, they took their inspiration from Eyam.

Penistone
On the Barnsley to Manchester road, the A628.
Erected on the second Sunday in June and blessed on the same day.
One only well dressed.

Wath-upon-Dearne
On the A633 Barnsley to Rotherham road.
A dressing was held here for the Millennium 2000 depicting "Christ and the women at the well". It was designed by a local artist, Sheila Thompson, and the work was supervised by Irene Hartley of Wickersley.
It was located close to the door of the parish church of All Saints near to the location of a lost well on Well Lane.
The donations were dedicated to Water Aid.

Wickersley
Off the A631 Rotherham to Maltby road.
A dressing was held here to commemorate the Millennium 2000 undertaken under the supervision of Irene Hartley (see Wath-upon-Dearne).
It was located at the Methodist Church.

GREATER MANCHESTER AND CHESHIRE

Adlington Hall
East of the A523 Macclefield to Hazelgrove road.
No details available.
Organised by the Adlington Civic Society, well dressing started here in 1990.
These boards were loaned to the Sutton Lane Ends dressers.

Chadkirk Chapel, Romily as for Gee Cross.
Erected on the last Saturday of July and blessed on the same day.
One well dressed.
Demonstrations available in the Chadwick Chapel.

Gee Cross
Hyde on the Stockport to Glossop road, the A560.
Erected on the second Sunday in July and blessed on the same day.
Three wells are dressed here:

Arnold Hill Well	Children of Dowson Primary School
Slateacre Road Well	Children of the Holy Trinity School
Booth's Well	Members of the Gee Cross Women's Institute

Sutton Lane Ends
South south-east of Macclesfield.
Erected second Saturday in July.
The first dressing here was held in 2001 and was organised by Sutton St James Church Pre-school Play Group using a main board and a children's board. The design was made and the dressing team led by Eddie and Wendy Davis having had 45 years of experience between them at Eyam, Derbyshire. The board was borrowed from Adlington Civic Society.

High Legh
On the Knutsford to M6 Junction 20 road.
Erected on the second Saturday of May and blessed the same day.

Macclesfield
On the Manchester to Leek road, the A523.
Erected on the second Saturday in July and blessed on the same day.

GLOUCESTERSHIRE

Bisley
North of Chalford on the Stroud to Cirencester road, the A419, on the south side of the church.
Seven Wells.
Erected on Ascension Day.

   This dressing was instigated by the Rev. Thomas Keble in 1863 after he had tidied the water supply system in the Wells road to the village. A service is held in the church and a procession is made to the wells where metal frames having wreaths and posies are laid. The twenty-two eldest pupils of the Bluecoat Village School carry the garlands and wreaths but their centrepiece is the carrying of Stars of David, the letters AD and the year, the letters spelling ASCENSION and five hoops. This must be unique amongst well dressings.

   The well (or wells) comprise five gabled shoots and one trough each side making seven wells. Pevsner stated that it was "rural and pretty, and useful for providing drinking water".

NORTH LINCOLNSHIRE

Caistor
Four well dressings were erected on 29th July 2000 as part of the Millennium celebrations. The designs celebrated the history of the town and featured:

   a) Caistor's Roman Centurion
   b) The devastating fire of Caistor
   c) England's largest Sheep Fair
   d) The Broken Cross and the Risen Christ

There are no plans for any further Well Dressings.

SHROPSHIRE

Betchcot, Parish of Smethcot.
Erected on 14 May.
A roadside well was decorated with flowers until the early years of the 20th century.

SOMERSET

Paulton
Located on the outskirts of the village.
Two wells dressed in 2000.
The Paulto (sic) Spring was also dressed in 1987.

WEST YORKSHIRE

Walton
East of Wetherby.
St Helen's Well, now covered. No details available.

Two wells dressed at Paulton, Somerset, 2000

Below: The Horse Trough, Old Hall Lane, Mayfield, showing an unusual design of well dressing in 2000

Opposite page: A Second Century Roman Centurion in the Market Place, Caistor, Lincolnshire

CLOOTIE, CLOUTIE AND RAG WELLS

See chapter three for more information about some of these wells.

OXFORDSHIRE

Oxford
St Edmund's Well near Oxford was dressed early in the 20th century, being mentioned by Firth in 1905.

CORNWALL

Carn Brae
Chapel Euny Holy Well, a short distance from Carn Euny, use the car park at Chapel Carn Euny and follow the track.
A clootie well.
Perpetual.

Penzance
St Madern or Madron's Well, north of the road from Penzance to St Just, the A3071.
A clootie well.
Perpetual.

Sancreed
West of Penzance, north of the Penzance to Land's End road, the A30.
A clootie well.
Perpetual.
It has been reported that the local Methodists clear the clouties from this well.

SCOTLAND

Culloden Moor
North of the back road from Inverness to Nairn, the B9006, follow the signs.
A cloutie well.
First Sunday of May or perpetual!
This well is much visited but should not be confused with the nearby "Well of the Dead" near to the National Trust for Scotland Centre on this famous battle site.

Dunfermline, Fife.
Located at the end of the A823(M) and Junction 3 of the M90.
St Margaret's Well was dressed on its saint's day, 20th July, up to 1649 when it was stopped by the Kirk Sessions. This also happened elsewhere in Scotland.

Munlochy, Black Isle.
St Boniface's Well.
On the Tore to Fortrose road, the A832.
A cloutie well.
Perpetual.
This is heavily visited and is a strong custom. The Bords record that at one time there were in excess of 50,000 rags to be seen.

Troqueer, Kirkcudbright.
Near to the Islesteps.
St Queron's (or St Jergon's) well.
Many coins were found in the water dating back centuries. Rags are still tied to the nearby bushes.

WALES

Disserth, Radnorshire.
On a minor road between the B3458 and A483 Builth Wells Towels road.
Mistletoe is hung on a bush on New Years Day. A Celtic custom if ever there was one.

St Seiriol's Well
Penmon, Black Point, Ynys Mon (Anglesey) with St Seiriol's Island (Ynys Seiriol or Puffin Island) across the water.
The well, near the priory ruins, was enclosed in a building in the 18th century, traces of St Seiriol's hermitage are evident close by.
All manner of things are left by visitors including rags, cloths, wreaths, fruit, etc.
Perpetual.

Glamorgan and Dyfed

It is known that there are several wells in these counties which attract many visitors who share the tradition of casting flowers on the grass, stones and bushes near to the wells on Easter Sunday.

IRELAND

Devotees of the television series "Ballykissangel" may recall an episode when a visit was made to St Bridget's Well complete with rags tied to branches of trees which grow nearby. The village of Avoca was used for the filming.

Wart Well, Dunvigen, Co Londonderry.
This well is located near to the ruinous priory church in a ballaun and is sited under a hawthorn where rags are hung by pilgrims. This forms only part of a Celtic ritual involving the well and standing stones. The rags for this well are torn from one's clothing.
The name suggests that it is one of many wells whose water is supposed to clear skin warts.

St Ciaran's Well, Clanmacnoise, Co. Offaly.
This well-known well shares its site with many crosses, graves, churches and round towers.
A whitethorn tree is to one side of the well where pilgrims hang offerings on the trees and throw offerings onto the water.

St Columkille Well
Also St Columbkille, Colm, Colum and Colmcille.
Talaght a southern suburb of Dublin, near Orlagh in a field west of Mount Venus.
Pilgrims tie rags, ribbons and garlands on the branches of the thorn trees nearby.
It is said that the water from this well will not boil – it does!

St Kevin's Well
Glendalough, south of Dublin, east off the Dublin to Wicklow road, the N81.
Pilgrims call and leave cloths on trees.
St Kevin of Glendalough is also named St Coemgen.

Tamlaghtard, Bellarena, Co Londonderry.
Bishop Aidan's Well near to Bellarena Rail Station is located in the graveyard of a ruined church and a modern church where visitors tie rags to the branches of an overhanging tree.

Doon Well
Located on the Letterkenny to Dunfanagh road at Kilmacrennan, County Donegal, the N56.
Visitors leave rags and other offerings here.
Perpetual.

Tobar Isa Well
Located on the road from Clonmel to Tipping, County Tiperrary, the N24 where it crosses the N8 at Cahir, near to the Wishing Well Bed and Breakfast.
Visitors leave rags here.
Perpetual.

Further Information

Information is available from the following. The telephone numbers were correct at the time of writing, December 2001.

Tourist Information:
　　　Derbyshire Tourism Officer's Group – 01663 751 210; North East Derbyshire District Council – 01246 345 777/8; Derbyshire Tourist Information Centres – Ashbourne 01335 343666; Bakewell 01629 813227; Buxton 01298 25106; Matlock 01629 55082

Web pages in general:
Try entering "well dressing", "welldressing" or "WELL DRESSING". You will find with certain pages that you will be inundated with references for food dressings, sartorial dressings, etc., but sifting through these for well dressings will be rewarding.

www.freehost.nu/members/welldressing/dates2
www.apusapus.demon.co.uk/ailsa/England/welldres
www.peakleisure.co.uk/well dressing in derbyshire
www.nbs.ntu.ac.uk/staff.shirors/wells
www.shef.ac.uk/english/natcect/weldress Sheffield University National Centre for English Cultural Tradition
www.lathkil.demon.co.uk/locevent

Web pages specific to well dressings and other sources and people far too numerous to mention individually to whom the authors offer their gratitude:

Bakewell:	*Well Dressings in Derbyshire*, Christian R., 1987
Barlow:	ibid.
Belper:	*History of Sutton in Ashfield*, Ed: Naylor P J., 1907
Betchcot:	*Shropshire Folk Lore* p 414
Bradwell:	www.bradda.peakisp.co.uk/vzone/wells/index
Bisley:	www.glscc.gov.uk/comm/index
	Sacred Waters, Bord and Bord, 1985
	Guide to Traditional Customs of Britain, Shuel B., 1985
Bonsall:	www-website.lineone.net/-wtimperley/page4.html
Bradley:	*History and Topography of Ashbourne and the Valley of the Dove*, Anon, 1839
Buxton:	www.buxtononline.net/Buxton-Online98/spa/test
	www.indigogroup.co.uk/edge/buxton
	Notes regarding St Anne's Well. Notes regarding St Anne's Well.
	Christian op cit
Buxworth:	www.navigationinn.co.uk/well-dressing
	Peak District Magazine, September 2000
Culloden:	www.tartans.com/beltaine
Derby:	www.derbycity.com/beltaine
	Christian op cit
Dore:	www.homepages.shu.ac.uk/~acsdry/wells
Elton:	*Insight Greenwatch*, July 2001
Endon:	*Victoria County History, Staffordshire*, p 180
	The Old Road to Endon, Ed. Speake R., 1974
Etwall:	www.etwall.demon.co.uk/wells
	Christian op cit
Eyam:	www.cix.co.uk/-dis/eyam98

Gee Cross: www.geecross.com/welldress
Great Longstone: www.fp.pussinbooots.plus.com/school
Heath: Christian op cit
Hope: ibid
Inverness: In Litt. Eileen MacAskill, Inverness Field Club
Lichfield: www.saintchads.org.uk/welldressinggallery
The Book of Saints 4th Edition 1947
Litton: Christian op cit
Matlock: In Litt. Dr Doreen Holden
Mayfield: *Ashbourne News*, 3rd July 1896
Middleton by Youlgreave:
Bugle 2000, Ed: Yuoatt E.,
Millthorpe: Christian op cit
Monyash: ibid
Norton: ibid
Pilsley: ibid
Riber: www.pealing.clara.net/rwd/main
Roston: *Highways and Byways of Derbyshire*, Firth J B., 1905
Rudyard: *Victoria County History, Staffordshire*, p 69

Rushton: ibid page 225
Rowsley: Christian op cit
Sutton Lane Ends: www.website.lineone.net/
~madriam/wells/sutton

Tintwhistle: www.thereviewonline.com/retro/
wdressing.

Tissington: www.derbyshireguide.co.uk/travel/
tissington
www.derbyshireuk.net/tiss
Waingroves: www.waingroves4.freeserve.co
West Hallam: www.23greenlane.freeserve.co.uk/
Page206
Whitwell: www.waynee.co.uk/well
Wormhill: Christian op cit

The persons who responded to our questionnaire:

Brackenfield	Nigel Rogers
Bradwell	Dorothy Crookes
Chapel-en-le-Frith	Mike Smith
Chelmorton	B H Clarke
Dore	Anne Slater
Elmton	Mrs P Finch
Etwall	Paul Cullen
Eyam	Francine Clifford
Holymoorside	Penny Brookes
Marston Montgomery	D Randall
Mayfield	Sara Maslauskas
Stoney Middleton	Michael Miller
Newborough	Isabel Davis
Tideswell	P C Fletcher
Upper Langwith	P Hoyland
Wormhill	V Barry Peirson
Youlgreave	Peter Pimm

to whom the publisher and authors offer their gratitude.

Wormhill, near Buxton, 1998

Occasionally well dressers are asked to make a well dressing for a special event, not connected with either the group they work with or an annual well dressing ceremony. One such person is Don Hughes of Wirksworth, Derbyshire who gained most of his expertise over many years when working on the Gatehouse Well in Wirksworth.

The following are some of the "special events" well dressings Don was involved in, together with his wife Jill, family and friends.

Lindow Man

The 2000 years old human body of a Celtic sacrifice was found at Lindow Moss near Wilmslow, Cheshire in 1984 in a peat digging. The oxygen free peat had preserved his corpse which is almost complete above the waist. This caused a great stir with the public and historians for he had obviously been sacrificed, as a ligature was still in place about his neck.

This was not the first such find, there have been many both in the United Kingdom, Denmark and elsewhere, except that this one was special for what it represented and for its excellent state of preservation.

It was placed in a dedicated exhibition at The Manchester Museum where it drew crowds of interested people. The curator decided that this corpse represented two important factors: the sanctity of water to the Celts and the cult of the head. (1)(2)

As part of the exhibition the museum decided to embellish the display with a well dressing of a Celtic cross in order to emphasise the Celtic tradition of water worship and their art. This created several problems, the chief of which was finding a method to make the materials more durable to survive the length of the exhibition. Instead of clay, a non-setting compound as used by glaziers was substituted and was smoothed over the frame to the traditional depth of 25 mm. The frame had already had 310 nails hammered into it.

The panel was protected with "cling film" and the design was pricked through the paper design into the compound at regular intervals. After peeling the design and the "cling film" off, the tiny pricks were joined together by using a needle, like a large "dot to dot" exercise.

The traditional method of pressing petals into the clay could not be relied upon, so wood glue was used where necessary. Fresh petals were discounted because they would shrivel and the colours are fugitive. The solution to the problem was to use non-perishable materials including dried hydrangea petals and pumpkin seeds, laid like tiles on a roof from the bottom of the board upwards.

The final result was most striking as the photograph shows and much interest was shown in it.

The exhibition opened on 25th March, 1991. The same evening Lindow Harmony, part of a larger choir originally formed in 1828, gave a concert of songs having themes linked to Celtic lore. (3)

The whole exhibition which was a great success was sponsored by the Pilkington Glass company, who are to be commended for their support. The Pilkington logo, almost Celtic in design, formed part of the dressing.

Lindow Man (affectionately dubbed Pete Marsh) is now in the British Museum, London where he has a special display.

The time taken and the materials used are given here as an example of how much it takes to dress a simple and small board:

56 person hours of work excluding the manufacture of the board
20 kg Butyl 66 non-setting compound
1560 pieces maize corn
1500 pumpkin seeds
480 coffee beans
380 dried hydrangea petals
220 sunflower seeds
90 dried camomile flowers
1 lb millet seed of which half fell off
half a bucket of grey and black lichen, which grows on walls
numerous squeezes of wood glue

and not to be ignored:

much patience
many cups of tea and coffee (4)

1) Manchester Museum exhibition leaflet 1991
2) *Celtic Derbyshire*, Naylor P J., 1983
3) Lindow Man private view leaflet 1991
4) Don Hughes' archive

Toyota Motor Manufacturing Ltd

In November, 1991, Derbyshire County Council organised a Derbyshire Japan Festival at Derby. This was to commemorate the successful establishment of their United Kingdom factory at nearby Burnaston. Mackworth College was the venue and the Japanese played a major role in this event.

A well dressing was offered as a contribution to the event which was happily accepted by the organisers. Design motifs were requested from Japan and, using these, a design was established having a strong Japanese flavour. The dressing was undertaken in situ and visitors were encouraged to help.

The dressing displayed the motif "YOUKOSO" which is Japanese for "welcome" with the well-known Toyota logo of three ellipses.

After the exhibition closed the dressing was transferred to and displayed in the Administration Building, Burnaston site.

J R R Tolkien

The anniversary of the birth of John Ronald Reuel Tolkien (1892-1973) was commemorated jointly by the Tolkien Society and the Mythopoeic Society in 1992, during a week of lectures and performances at the Centenary Conference attended by enthusiasts from all over the world.

The society requested floral tributes for laying at the joint grave of J R R Tolkien and his wife at Oxford, at which university he was a professor. Tolkien named himself as "Beren" and his wife Edith as "Luthian", for which names he had designed motifs, which were used as the basis of two dressings, to be placed either side of their gravestone.

The two dressings were made and delivered to Oxford where they were exhibited in Keble College Chapel during a thanksgiving service on 23rd August, 1992, the final event of this conference. The service was taken by the Rev. Stephen Tucker, Dean of Divinity at New College together with Father Robert Murray, S.J., afterwards the dressings were taken to the grave at Wolvercote Cemetery where they were seen by members of the conference during the day.

Festival of Workshops for Schools

This festival took place on Tuesday, 25th May, 1993, at Derby Cathedral, the theme being Industrial Heritage and the occasion being a Schools' Workshop Day in Music, Arts and Crafts.

A board was designed and prepared and under supervision it was dressed by pupils from Hartshorne, Weston, Newbold, Hartington, Fritchley and College Primary Schools.

The dressing featured industrial scenes from the past, including: mill stones, the Wirksworth medieval lead miner, a steam locomotive, coal mine headstocks, terraced industrial housing with miners setting off for work, the Cat and Fiddle post mill, bottle kilns and iron furnaces.

Hampton Court Palace

The flower show organised by the Royal Horticultural Society held each year at the Hampton Court Palace is a magnet for garden and plant lovers from far and wide.

The July, 1996 show was no exception other than in this year a well dressing was exhibited. The theme was "All things bright and beautiful" and featured Derbyshire White and Dark Peak, scenes including: mill stones, High Tor, Wirksworth church, the Monsal Dale clapper bridge, houses on the Causeway at Wirksworth, Haddon Hall, Black Rocks, stone walled fields and open moors with a glimpse of the Derwent Reservoir, all under a partly sunlit, partly clouded sky. The space for this was provided by Hardy's Cottage Garden Plants of Laverstoke, Hampshire (Gold Medallists at Chelsea, 1996) who funded the project. It drew crowds of spectators and much attention. Many more people were now aware of well dressing because of this. Robert Hardy hails from Clifton, Ashbourne, Derbyshire. His brother-in-law described it as being "quite spectacular".

The periodical, "Garden New", dated 24-30 July, 1996 commented, "It was the first time that a well dressing had been seen in the south and a stream of fascinated visitors viewed the display."

Team Spirit

The magazine of the Wirksworth Team Ministry, centred on the Parish Church of St Mary, Wirksworth, has a Celtic emblem on its front cover.

In the millennium year of 2000, it was decided to create a circular well dressing using this emblem. The result was stunning due to its beautiful design enhanced by the inspirational choice of colours. It was located on the floor directly beneath the tower.

The materials used are of interest as certain of them were unusual: white tape to commemorate that Wirksworth was a chief manufacturer of tapes in the Kingdom, fossils and limestone from local quarries, a major source of employment locally, and galena or lead ore to recall that the mining of this and other metal ores was the chief industry of the parish for centuries.

The ingredients were:

Outer circle:	Parsley, lovage, cow parsley flowers
Centre circle:	An ammonite and crinoid fossils set in galena chippings
Celtic cross:	Limestone chippings
Celtic knots:	White tape
Dark Green:	Box leaves
White ring:	Chrysanthemum centres
Yellow ring:	Chrysanthemum petals
Yellow circles:	Chrysanthemum centres
White rings:	Ditto
Black outlining:	Wool – three strands twisted together
"Jigsaw" pieces:	Lovage and small green pine cones

Perth, Western Australia

Don Hughes also helped to set up the permanent well dressing housed in the Wirksworth Heritage Centre in Crown Yard, off the Market Place, and was indirectly involved in the first well dressing ceremony in Perth, Western Australia, on Australia Day, 26 January, 1985. (See chapter two for more information on the Heritage Centre).

The first Australian well dressing was initiated by Tom Shaw, an Englishman from Rawdon Street, Derby who eventually emigrated to Australia. In 1984, after he had retired, Tom was irritated by a statement made on the radio on Australia Day, suggesting that our English Midland shires had nothing as interesting as the Scottish bagpipes and Morris dancing performed in the south of the country.

Tom protested to his locals citing the tradition of well dressing practised in Derbyshire, one of the "shires". He explained to those who would listen about the beauty and complexity of this art and the locals then challenged him to show them one of these dressings.

Tom decided to write (mainly on audio cassette tapes) to England for advice and he was put in touch with Clarence Daniel, the late Eyam historian, and Don Hughes. (Tom had visited Wirksworth as a child, to see his Grandmother.) Don sent him the full written instructions on how to make a well dressing, together with slides of Wirksworth well dressings, showing every stage of the process.

Tom enlisted the help of locals and the idea of a well dressing started to look like a possibility. The chemist at a local brickworks created a method for retarding the effects of heat on clay and a mining company helped with water. Many volunteers worked on the single dressing under Tom's tuition and the result was most acceptable, Tom had made his point.

The dressing was displayed at the base of Mount Eliza in King's Park, Perth and two hymns special to the Eyam dressings were sung at a service in a Perth church.

Tom took slides of well dressings on a lecture tour of Australia, New Zealand and Tasmania. One wonders if any of this rubbed off and are there dressings in the Antipodes of which we have no knowledge? Tom died in 1994, but did well dressing live on in Perth?

Acknowledgement is made to an article in the Derby Evening Telegraph dated Thursday, 26 September, 1985. *Source:* Don Hughes' personal archive.

Opposite page: The Perth Well which shows Captain Stirling who claimed Perth for the Empire in 1827

APPENDIX: INGREDIENTS

This list is gleaned from the responses to an enquiry sent by the publisher to a number of well dressing committees.

It is intended to be both a matter of interest to the reader and as a guide for would-be new dressers. Common names only have been used.

Clay

Clay can be had from various places:
> Local quarry
> Under the topsoil in alluvial land
> Banks of streams

Local pottery – you may have to pay

Remember to obtain the land owner's permission first for clay removal from fields, etc. You MUST co-operate with the quarry manager when taking clay. Quarries are dangerous places.

Some dressers reconstitute the clay from year to year by storing in polythene bags and adding water to rejuvenate it. This method takes much puddling and can be very hard work.

The popular thickness for the clay is 25 mm, but some dressings work on clay having a thickness varying from 25 mm to 50 mm.

Wetting

There are several favoured methods:
> Immersing in a pond or stream for several days
> Hose pipe for an hour or so
> Splashing from a bucket

One speculates why there is such a wide variance in methods from soaking for several days to splashing. The dressers who use the latter method never seem to have any trouble with premature drying out. At least one dressing prefers not to wet their frames.

Outlines

Plant material:

Petals inserted, Sweet Cicely, Reeds, Alder "cones", Wheat straw

Seeds:

Maize (Sweet Corn), Coffee beans, Coriander, Aniseed, Poppy, black and white Peppercorns

White:

Carnation, Chrysanthemum, Cotton Grass, Geranium, Gerbera, Dianthus, Honesty, Hydrangea, Margarites, Moon, Oxeye Daisy, Philadelphus, Sedum, Spa (white calcite), Statice, Sweet William

Black:

Alder cones, Aniseed seeds, Aquilegia seeds, Banana skins, Coal, Lichen (reverse side), Moss (reverse side), Senna pods, slate, tree bark

Blue:

Blue is a problem colour as certain blue petals are fugitive especially the Harebell.

Bluebells, Cornflower, Cranes Bill, Harebell, Hydrangea, Lavender, Lobelia, Delphinium, Periwinkle, Statice

Green:

Cacti, Conifer leaves, Cotoneaster, Creeping Jenny, Cupressus cones, Delphinium, Dock, Eucalyptus leaves, Herbs (Kitchen), Hydrangea, Lady's Mantle, Moss, Parsley, Privet, Sycamore, Rhubarb "seeds" (these are actually the flower buds), foliage

Yellow:

Alyssum, Anthemis, Aster, Buttercups, Calendula, Carnation, Chrysanthemum, Daffodil, Gerbera, Geum, Golden Privet, Maize, Marigold, Millet seed (birds eat it), Potentilla, Sedum, Stallion, Stonecrop, Wallflower

Red:

Carnation, Geranium, Gerbera, Geum, Hydrangea, Potentilla, Sage (red), Sweet William, Wallflower, Zinnia

Brown:

Bark, Berberis, Birch dust, Bulrush (Reed Mace), Catkin (ex Willow), Copper Beech leaves, Dock seed, Fir cones, Hydrangea (dried flowers), Laurel leaves, Montbretia, Moss, Rhubarb leaves (dried), Sedum (dried), Wallflower

Orange:

Buddleia, Calendula, Carnation, Chrysanthemum, Gerbera, Geum, Lentils, Marigold, Orange (the fruit), Tagetes, Wallflowers

Non plant miscellaneous:

Egg shells, hair (human, dog, etc), feathers, fur, pebbles, sea shells, stone

It is known that spray paint has been used on a dressing – naughty!

Note:

One of the pleasures of well dressing is the hunt for materials. Look for leaves and flowers in your own garden or in the countryside, but do not take wild flowers which are now protected by Act of Parliament. One can but try with a new found leaf or flower; however, they do not always succeed.

The annual custom of well dressing begins a couple of weeks before Ascension Day. The frames are brought out of storage and the old clay, still adhering to the boards, is removed. They are then placed in the village pond to fully soak the frames.

The clay for all the frames is obtained from a nearby field and divided between the various wells. The frames are dressed in the Tissington Hall stables and various barns or shippons, as they are known locally, in the village. Sometimes frames may be prepared together. In 1997 for example, Coffin and Yew Tree Wells were dressed together at Town Head Farm.

While the frames are soaking thoughts turn towards collecting the raw materials that are required, although flowers are left until later. The borders for the flowers are outlined with coffee beans or "black nobs" – the cones from alder trees. The latter have to be collected in their hundreds and are used on Yew Tree Well. Other materials such as beech mast, beech leaves, seeds, sand etc can be obtained in advance. Recently, clay has been obtained from near Tissington Wood Farm. It is dug out by five men and a quantity dropped off at each well.

Over the weekend prior to Ascension Day, the clay is puddled – mixed with water and trodden in old baths etc. It becomes more malleable, and stones and dead leaves are removed, before the clay is applied to the frames. Salt is added to prolong the softness.

About an inch of clay is applied to the boards which are covered with nails to give rigidity to the clay. It is then smoothed down with a plasterer's trowel. All the frames are different and clay has to be applied to the different panels.

For Town Well, these have the following names: the main board in the middle that contains the picture is known as the picture or summer board. There are both inner and outer columns. The board containing the inscription is the head board. The Town Well has a crown – a circular board which fits into the top of the head board. The latter is known as the letter board by Wendy Greatorix who currently designs Hand's Well. The dressing of the wells takes three days – usually Monday to Wednesday. The bare outline of the design is drawn on sheets of paper which are lain on the smooth surface of the clay. The outlines are pricked through into the clay using something like a cocktail stick and the holes are about $1/2$ inch apart.

Previous page: The frames are soaked prior to applying the clay. This is to reduce drying out of the clay. The boards are loosely tied together with string so they can be easily retrieved from the village pond

Left: Treading the clay to make it malleable. Stones and roots have to be removed and water added to obtain the right consistency. Left is Mark Aldous and right is Ken Hodgkinson. Sir Richard FitzHerbert (in hat) lends a hand and in this case, his feet

Above: Salt (in the white bag) is also added to reduce drying out

At this point, all the main elements are being assembled. Hydrangeas and bluebells, daisies, carnations, statice, moss, yew, parsley, rhubarb seeds, – the list goes on according to the requirements of the well designers. Incredibly, there is no conferring between designers and apparently only once has the same theme been used simultaneously. Other methods are used to create the image in the clay, for example, templates of letters give the outline for words or circles may have to be drawn.

The boards are then ready for dressing. They are laid out in what can be cold and draughty sheds, the dressers seeming oblivious to the circumstances. To the outsider, the scene can appear almost bizarre: sheets hanging down the front of a wall of hay to prevent grass from dropping onto the designs; children, including some very young ones, deftly and expertly applying petals to wet clay under the watchful eye of an equally hard working mum; delicate and beautiful designs being developed in a cramped stall recently vacated by a cow; a quiet confidence that all will be ready by Wednesday night.

Some families have been engaged for generations – the Bailey family can claim five – and one can be sure this is not unique. Once a board's outline is finished, the job of creating the outline begins with coffee beans or black nobs being used in considerable quantities. Once outlined, the delicate job of dressing can begin.

Although many flower heads or petals are small, it is surprising how quickly the design progresses. The stalks of small flower heads – such as statice or daisies are pressed into the clay. Some petals, such as hydrangea, or whole flowers such as bluebells, are pressed in flat. The use of some contrasting colours can create quite strong designs, such as a white cross on a background of dark blue bluebells.

While well dressing work goes on the villagers mow lawns, erect signs on the Ashbourne to Buxton road and prepare the church.

During Wednesday afternoon the final touches are applied to the boards – a touch of pressure on a petal here, a spray of hair lacquer there. After tea, the boards are taken out and carefully erected over the wells. They are usually left for a week, but in one very damp year, they were left up until the end of the second weekend.

Methods of erecting the boards vary; the head or letter board is jointed into columns. Installation is awkward and more time-consuming at Coffin Well because it is in a garden. The letterboard is held above the columns (until they are positioned correctly) on a large hook tied off onto a branch in the tree above. The Hand's Well team have a special metal frame which is attached to the front of the arms of a tractor.

Top: When the clay is of the right consistency, it is carried indoors to the frames, where it is applied to the right thickness by Rupert Barrington (middle) and David Newall (bottom)

This lifts the head frame into the air and supports it until it is dropped down onto the columns. The picture board on Town Well fits inside the stone built well hood and the columns are completely separate and stand slightly in front with the head board sitting on the top of the stonework. Hall Well is by far the largest, fitting inside the large stone surround to the well.

In all cases, the frames have to be supported so that they do not fall over.

There is of course more work to be done beyond this more obvious 'behind the scenes' activity. Ronald Daybell, Chairman of the Ashford-in-the-Water Well Dressing Committee seemed to sum it all up rather well in this quote from the 1997 commemorative leaflet:

"Behind the Petals

As you look at our Well Dressings, have you ever wondered what goes on behind the scenes? Here in our small village everybody can be involved in our festival who wants to be, and any 'incomers' are invited (or press-ganged) to help. Apart from the last-minute drawing of pictures and begging-borrowing-stealing of suitable petals, there are many other vital aspects...

'Red tape' formalities involve a street-collection permit, police permission for the procession and arrangements for parking, and Public Liability Insurance (now costing almost £100) is a 'must'; less formal but still vital arrangements need to be made to book the band and to choose hymns for each well suitable for the picture's theme and also for playing outside (and preferably to tunes already held in the Band's music-store, because new music is prohibitively expensive). We certainly couldn't do our petalling without clay, which is no longer easy to come by (and we are grateful to the Hanson Brick Company for donating this again this year), or a 'tame' joiner who will repair any damaged well-boards.

Where our wells are floodlit, we are dependent upon nearby householders for allowing us to connect up to their power supply and this couldn't be done without the services of a kind electrician. The boards need to be stored between-times, and take up a lot of space; our thanks to 'The Grange' for use of its stables. Other people kindly allow advertisement-boards to be sited on their property – the boards need to be re-dated, erected, taken down again and stored. Then there is our 'Heavy Gang' who transport the boards before and after claying, erect the petalled pictures and transport the stripped boards away again – long may they survive slipped discs! – there are the ropes to sort out and the money boxes to fasten on, the Treasurer must empty these regularly (we have had thefts, particularly from the tucked-away Children's Well boxes) and count the cold, sometimes wet and sticky, coins and manhandle it to the bank...(and submit accounts to support our application for our next street collection permit).

After the event, we meet to decide which charities shall share our 'takings' and then we try to catch up with housework and gardens, perhaps even holidays; soon after Christmas, somebody says "Have you thought about your well yet?" The programme editor says "The write-ups for the magazine need to be in by the end of January this year". In a state of shock the Secretary has to be dragged out of hibernation by the Chairman and start at the end of the red tape all over again!"

The preparation of the well boards is a fairly quick process in Tissington – three full days and they are finished. Elsewhere, wells are only dressed in the evenings after work and the process can take a week to complete. Monyash is an example of this. Availability of certain colours can clearly be a problem. In one year they ran out of blue and had to strip the side panels to find sufficient petals for the picture board. It has not been unknown for white flowers to be sprayed blue as an emergency measure by one village.

It is strange how much reverence we bestow on ancient customs. Well dressing is now very popular in Derbyshire and it attracts significant numbers of visitors, raising a lot of money for various charitable purposes. Yet it hasn't always been this way. At the beginning of the 19th century, the custom had died out in the county except at Tissington.

It is remarkable that this ancient tradition, originating many hundreds of years ago and perhaps having its origins in pre-Christian times, should survive through the efforts of one Derbyshire village. Coincidentally, another custom previously observed in many places around the country – Shrovetide mass football – survives only in one town, Ashbourne, and that is five miles from Tissington. Whilst a regeneration of mass football played through the streets would no doubt cause considerable alarm outside Ashbourne, the revival of well dressing has been met with considerable approval.

Despite the proliferation of villages and towns dressing their ancient wells or even preparing boards where a well does not survive, Tissington is still regarded as the mother of well dressing, as a journalist described it fifty years ago. It is still the first of the Peak District villages to dress its wells of spring water. This used to mean that the colours were not as bright as later dressings, because it was too early for some colourful wild flowers, but cultivated flowers are also now used.

Opposite page: Flowers stand ready for the dressers as the clay is applied to the boards of Hall Well

Top Right: Mrs Joan Leeds at work on a side panel

Above: Mrs Carole Unwin and Kelly Greatorex (daughter of Hand's Well designer Wendy) get the petalling underway

Dressed at Home Farm. After marking the clay with a template, and outlining the design, the petals start to be laid down in a shippon (or cowshed). Once complete, the boards are taken to the well on the Wednesday evening

Above: The head board awaits ground calcite to provide the white back-ground before being taken by tractor (below) to the well; Right: The head board awaits the assembly of the framework so that it may be dropped into place under the watchful eye of David Boam

Assembly of the side boards. The tractor has a special attachment to carry the head board. Designer Wendy Greatorex is top left. Mark Naylor (in yellow jacket) checks that the side board is in the correct position

The completed well. The white background of crushed calcite comes from Long Rake Spa Co., near Friden

THE FIRST ARCHBISHOP OF CANTERBURY

SAINT AUGSTINE

1400TH ANNIVERSARY

1400TH ANNIVERSARY

With the outline completed with coffee beans, Lady Caroline FitzHerbert
(top right) and Alice Shields (above) start work on this large set of boards.
Below: Sarah Muirhead completes another flower motif

Note the design sheet hanging from the wall (top right) as Lucie-Claire Watson lends a helping hand.
The baskets of loaves and fishes near completion (below)

It is Tuesday and Mrs Tucker (left) and Jo Lichfield continue the petalling

Opposite page: Sir Richard FitzHerbert oversees the erection of the board as night-time falls. Helping is Ted Hickmott and at far right, Martin Froggatt, who usually helps with the erecting of Hall Well

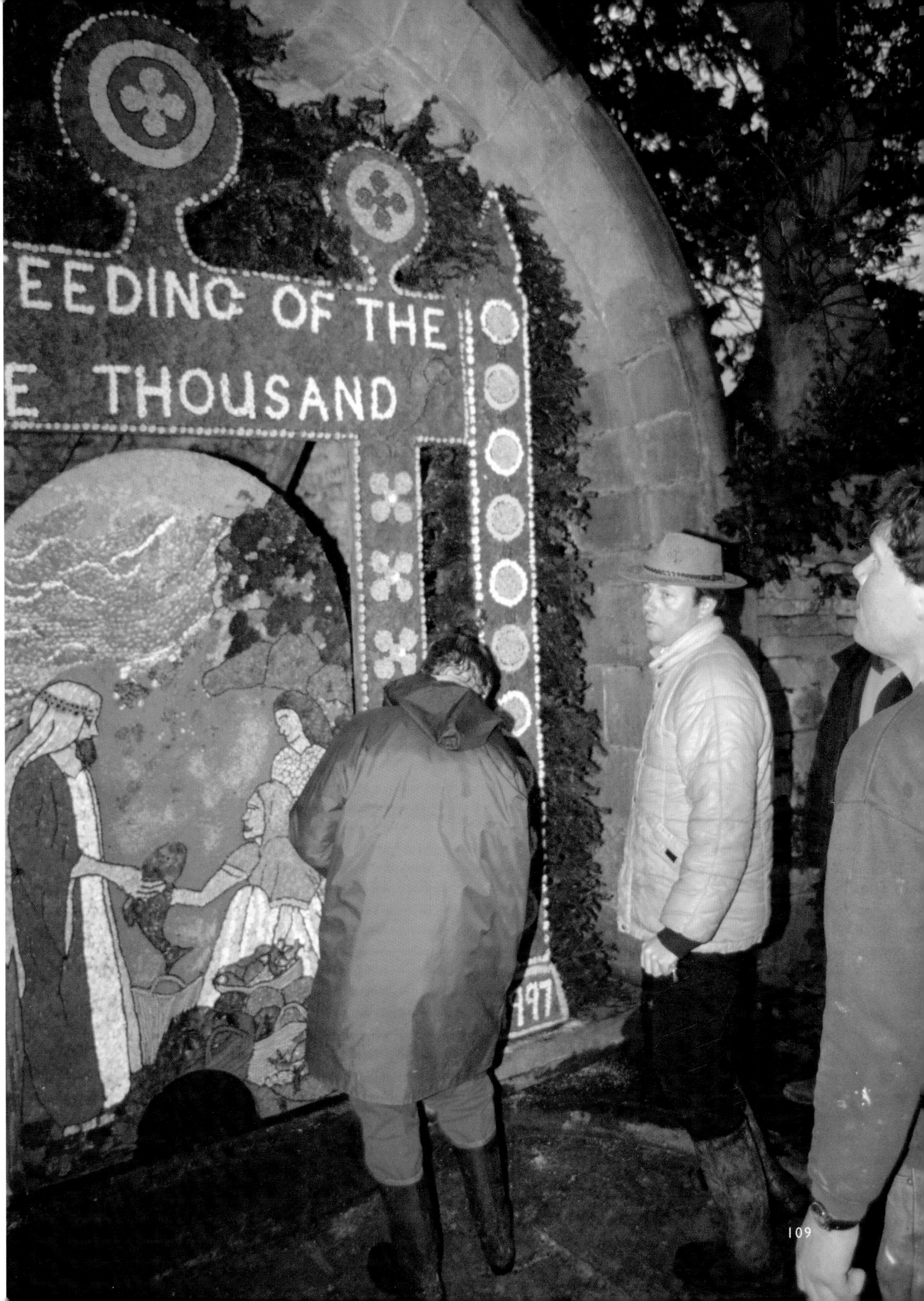
EEDING OF THE
E THOUSAND

The blessing of the well

It is Monday and work gets underway on Town Well which is dressed at Wibbern Hill Farm.
Lending a hand are Mary (left) and Rosalyn Bagguley

As work starts on one board (page 111) another, outlined with coffee beans, is ready for dressing.
Christine Wheeldon (below) at work on the central panel. Five generations of her family (the Baileys) have dressed Town Well

Left: Louise Bartram and Victoria Bailey putting down rhubarb flowers on a side board

Below: By Wednesday night the boards are completed and erection begins at the well. Oliver Watson makes a final adjustment to the picture or summer board

It is getting dark and the rain starts to pour. With Ascension Day the following morning, work has to proceed regardless

Fitzherbert Primary
School
Garden Party
Sunday 18th May 2pm
at Fenny Bentley Hall
Attractions
Duck Race
Ashbourne Town Band
display by
Beavers

Left: Eleanor Naylor (left) chatting to Ann Naylor and Laura Bissel (right) as outlining proceeds on the inner board surround. Petalling begins at Town Head Farm as soon as the outline is done, using traditional alder cones (called "black nobs") rather than coffee beans. The two sheets (left) prevent straw blowing onto the designs. Below: Valerie Bostock (left) watches Dianne Wilton (right) and Laura Bissel working on the right hand panel

Opposite page: Valerie Bostock, the Coffin Well Co-designer, pricking out the design

Below: Kath Burton, the Co-designer of the well, completes the headboard with bluebells

Erecting the boards is more complicated because of the shape of the well and its position in a garden rather than at the roadside. A ladder is required as the head board is suspended from a tree branch. Doing the erecting work are Daniel and (?) Colin Naylor and Denis Stone

Opposite page: Coffin Well is the only north-facing well in Tissington, which means it does not catch the sun and is usually in the shade

The Children's Well is dressed alongside Hall Well at the Hall stables. Here are the early stages of dressing with the many helping hands of the next generation of petallers

The completed board in the stable and later, lying on the grass verge after dark awaiting erection (top). All things bright and beautiful before the first visitors on Ascension Day morning

Opposite page; Top left: From left to right, Esme Tressider, Robert and Samantha Bostock and Rebecca Eaton help the adults; Top Right: Mariana Sampson (left) and Claire Margison (right) highlight the text and border; Middle: Jacqui Luker depetals yellow carnations prior to pressing them into the clay

CHILDREN'S WELL

Above: A close up of "black nobs" being applied on the boards of Yew Tree Well (right) by Christopher Carr & Elaine Watson and Christopher Fry. The work is done at Town Head Farm; Below: Applying the petals to the main board

Above: Anne Callandine and daughter Helen Foggatty applying the petals to the main board
with the design sheet hanging on the wall; Below: Margaret Carr petalling the head board

Top left: Stephen Slone working on a side panel. Other photographs: Well boards awaiting erection as the rain stops

Opposite page: Yew Tree Well completed, with a border of hawthorn to keep children and pets from disturbing the arrangement

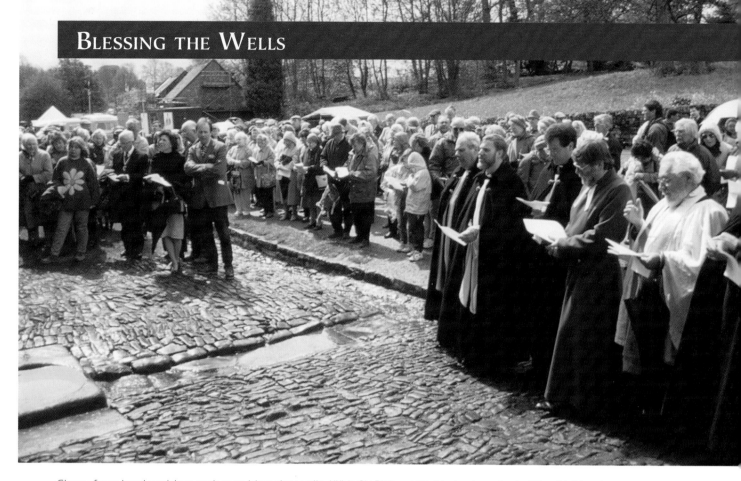

Clergy from local parishes gather to bless the wells. With Sir Richard FitzHerbert are Lady Olga Maitland, then MP for Sutton and a kinsman of Sir Richard, and Richard Perkins, High Sheriff of Derbyshire. These photographs were taken at the Hall Well